D1725045

IBIZA TRAVEL GUIDE 2024

Unveiling The Charms of Ibiza

Dennis M. Portet

TABLE OF CONTENTS

Chapter 1: Introduction to Ibiza

Ibiza, sometimes known as the "White Isle," is a gem in Spain's Balearic archipelago, tucked away in the azure embrace of the Mediterranean Sea. Pleasure-seekers from all over the world flock to this sun-drenched paradise, which is well-known for its alluring fusion of throbbing nightlife and tranquil natural beauty. The exuberant rhythms of the night give way to the peaceful serenades of dawn in Ibiza, where the ancient and the modern blend harmoniously.

An Ensemble of Past and Present

Ibiza has layers of millennia-old history beneath the vibrant exterior of beach parties and loud clubs. A patchwork of civilizations, influenced by Phoenician, Carthaginian, Roman, and Moorish elements, can be seen in the island's architecture, customs, and cuisine. Ibiza Castle stands guard, a testament to the island's legendary past, while the cobblestone lanes of Ibiza Town's Dalt Vila, a UNESCO World Heritage site, reverberate with whispers of bygone eras.

Nature's Canvas: The Beaches

Ibiza boasts more than 80 beaches along its coastline, each offering a unique landscape of sandy beaches. While the boisterous Playa d'en Bossa pulses to the beat of the island's dynamic nightlife, Cala Comte's clear waters and golden dunes are a testament to nature's artistic ability. The flamingos' sanctuary and sun-seekers dreamy backdrop are provided by the shimmering salt flats of Ses Salines, which lie to the south like diamonds.

A Musical Symphony

The beats of Ibiza's nocturnal carnival reverberate throughout the world at night. Famous nightclubs like Pacha, Amnesia, and Ushuaïa invite partygoers with the promise of amazing evenings beneath the starry canopy. Born in the hedonistic days of the 1970s, the island's music culture has developed into a worldwide phenomenon that attracts both electronic music aficionados and DJs.

Culinary Journey

The rich terroir of Ibiza is showcased in the island's delectable food scene. The island has everything for every epicurean taste, from Michelin-starred restaurants serving up cutting-edge cuisine to beachside chiringuitos serving fresh catch of the day. Sun-kissed food from local markets finds its way onto plates in colorful displays of Mediterranean fare, while local delicacies like Bullit de Peix and Sofrit Pagès entice palates with their genuine flavors.

A Wellness Sanctuary

Ibiza provides a haven for renewal and self-discovery beyond the partying. While luxurious spa resorts treat visitors to holistic treatments amid beautiful, fragrant gardens, yoga retreats built on cliffs overlooking the sea offer a peaceful setting for reflection. The island is a perfect location for holistic healing therapies because of its scenic beauty and serene atmosphere.

Ibiza displays its duality as the sun sets, illuminating the horizon with shades of pink and gold. It is a place that exudes both unending energy and tranquility in equal measure. At this location, historic stones tell secrets from the past, and the sea wind whispers of amazing experiences to come. A fresh experience can be found all across this island, luring visitors to immerse themselves in a setting where the pulse of life and the rhythms of nature coexist. For those who are fortunate enough to witness its charm, Ibiza, in all its radiant grandeur, is ready to leave a lasting impression.

Synopsis of the Island

Located in the center of the Balearic archipelago, Ibiza shines like a brilliant pearl in the Mediterranean Sea. Stretching just more than 40 kilometers from tip to tip, this captivating island is a colorful contrast-filled playground. Ibiza attracts tourists looking for a well-balanced mix of adventure and relaxation with its vibrant energy and well-known nightlife as well as the peaceful seclusion of its isolated coves.

Location and Topography

The varied geography of Ibiza features a charming combination of lush meadows, sloping hills, and towering cliffs that plunge into blue seas. An array of greens and blues creates a gorgeous symphony as pine-clad hillsides give way to secret beaches with fine sand. Salt flats, an essential habitat for migratory birds and a stark contrast to the throbbing energy in the north may be found on the island's southern shore.

Temperature and the Magnificence of Nature

Ibiza is blessed with a Mediterranean climate, meaning that most of the year is filled with sunny days. Summers run from June to September and are defined by warm weather that is ideal for swimming and tanning. The mild weather in the spring and fall is ideal for outdoor activities and exploration. Ibiza is a great place for people looking for a more peaceful getaway because it maintains its attractiveness throughout the winter with pleasant weather and fewer tourists.

The Conservation and Preservation of Biodiversity

Beyond its stunning beaches, Ibiza is known for its rich biodiversity, which flourishes in its pristine natural environments. A wide variety of plants and animals find refuge in pine forests, ponds, and meadows. Initiatives to protect the island's distinctive ecosystems demonstrate the island's dedication to sustainability and conservation. Ibiza's commitment to maintaining its natural legacy is demonstrated by protected sites like Es Vedrà Natural Reserve and Ses Salines Natural Park.

Integration of Cultures

Ibiza's historical tapestry is evident in its cultural landscape. The customs, architecture, and gastronomy of the island have been profoundly influenced by Phoenician, Carthaginian, Roman, and Moorish elements. The best example of this melting pot of cultures is seen in the UNESCO-listed Dalt Vila neighborhood of Ibiza Town, where quaint cafés and colorful stores coexist with historic fortifications.

A Draw to Expression and Creativity

Ibiza has long been a draw for musicians, artists, and free spirits in addition to its inherent charm. For many years, the island's captivating aura and stunning landscape have stimulated the imaginations of artists, resulting in a thriving artistic community and a constantly changing cultural environment.

There is a tale to be discovered, a view to be marveled at, and an instant to be treasured around every corner of Ibiza. This island extends an invitation to discover life in all its vibrant grandeur, whether one is drawn to the throbbing beats of the nightlife or the calming embrace of the natural world. With its alluring beauty, Ibiza promises a journey that is beyond time and deeply affects the soul of any traveler who is lucky enough to experience its magic.

The Historical Importance

Ibiza's story is told via a tapestry of civilizations that have woven their stories over the ages, each leaving their permanent imprint on the island. The history of Ibiza unfolds like the pages of an old book. The culture, architecture, and customs of this little Mediterranean gem have been shaped by millennia of human activity.

Footprints of Phoenicians

Among the first people to realize Ibiza's vital position in marine commerce routes were the adventurous seafarers of antiquity, the Phoenicians. They called their settlement "Ibossim," and they arrived on the island in the 7th century BCE. This early arrival marked the beginning of Ibiza's history and laid the foundation for later civilizations.

Punic Wars and Roman Rule

Ibiza was conquered by the Romans in 123 BCE as the Roman Republic grew in power. Because of its advantageous geographic position and abundant agricultural resources, the island experienced great wealth during the Roman era. Ibiza's strategic importance was further highlighted by the Punic Wars, a series of battles fought between Rome and Carthage in the waters surrounding the island.

Moroccan Heritage

The Moorish era came to an end when Ibiza was included in the vast area of the Umayyad Caliphate in the ninth century CE. This era produced agricultural advancements, architectural wonders, and a vibrant culture that forever changed the face of the island. In the winding lanes of Ibiza Town's ancient section, the alluring fusion of Moorish influences is still discernible.

Island Fortifications and Medieval Marauders

Ibiza went through a difficult time throughout the Middle Ages when it started to attract the attention of other Mediterranean nations. Robust defenses were built in response to the competition for dominance between opposing empires, privateers, and pirates. With its enormous stone walls and magnificent views serving as a silent witness to centuries of watchfulness, Ibiza Town's Dalt Vila, a UNESCO-listed citadel, is a testament to the island's strategic significance.

Contemporary Shift and Renaissance of Culture

Ibiza experienced a revolutionary resurgence in the 20th century. Attracted by its magnetic energy and beautiful panoramas, the island became a haven for artists, bohemians, and free spirits. Ibiza's longstanding image as a center of creativity and uniqueness around the world was established by the counterculture that was burgeoning in the 1960s and 1970s, which gave the island a spirit of artistic expression.

The vivid pulse of modern life is woven into Ibiza's historical tapestry, which is no longer limited to its old stones. Discover the layers of history that have shaped the island's captivating present by exploring its cobblestone streets and sun-drenched terraces, which all bear testament to the island's illustrious past. Because of its long history, Ibiza is a place where tradition, modernity, and time have all come together to create a seamless dance of cultural legacy.

Chapter 2: Getting to Ibiza

You may get to Ibiza's charms in a few different ways. Ibiza Airport welcomes foreign aircraft all year round and serves the island. Flying is an easy option because major European cities provide direct connections. If you'd prefer a more picturesque way to travel across the Mediterranean, boat services connect Ibiza to nearby islands and mainland Spain. Ferries traveling at high speed depart from places such as Valencia and Barcelona. A customized arrival experience can be had with private yachts and charter services, which add a hint of luxury. Taking any route will get to Ibiza, but getting there promises to be just the beginning of the colorful picture that this alluring Mediterranean jewel has in store.

Choices for Transport

Getting Around Ibiza by Car

Easy access to the island is made possible by Ibiza's well-organized transportation system. Ibiza has an array of choices to accommodate every traveler's inclination, be it the liberty of independent discovery or the convenience of guided tours.

One great way to see Ibiza at your own speed is by renting a car. From little automobiles for city trips to tough vehicles for off-road exploration, several rental companies have a wide selection of cars. Hidden coves, historical attractions, and picturesque overlooks are all easily accessible via the island's well-maintained road network. Booking ahead is crucial, though, particularly during the busiest travel times.

2. Renting a scooter or bicycle can be a more agile and environmentally responsible choice. This lets you find attractive corners and travel through small streets that might be impossible to reach by automobile. For cyclists, Ibiza is the perfect vacation because of its mild climate and mostly flat terrain.

3. Public Transit: The public transportation system in Ibiza is effective and well-connected. The island's main towns, beaches, and tourist destinations are connected by buses. Travelers on a tight budget will find the service to be dependable and a wise option. Real-time route and schedule information is also available via the Ibiza Bus app.

4. Taxis: Found all across the island, taxis are an easy way to get around and are a great option for short trips or for when you just want to relax and take in the view. In cities, you can find taxis at specific stands or by hailing one on the street.

Ibiza's stunning coastline makes boat and ferry services a popular option for mobility. Connecting Ibiza with nearby islands like Mallorca and Formentera are ferries and water taxis. One of the best ways to see the island's breathtaking coastline, quiet coves, and abundant marine life is to charter a boat or go on a guided trip.

Tourist trains and excursion buses: These modes of transportation provide instructive commentary while offering guided tours to well-known sites. Without having to worry about finding your way, these tours are a great way to explore Ibiza's historical landmarks, cultural legacy, and scenic beauties.

7. Private transports & Shuttles: Reserve private transports or shuttle services for a hassle-free experience arriving and departing. For parties or families in particular, these door-to-door options offer convenience.

Ibiza makes certain that every visitor can experience the island in a way that best suits their interests and goals by providing a wide range of transportation choices. Ibiza has a variety of opportunities to set out on an amazing adventure, whether your preference is for the independence of the open road, the peace of the sea, or the convenient guided tours.

Airports and Aircraft

The well-connected airport in Ibiza welcomes visitors from all over the world as the entryway to this Mediterranean paradise. An essential hub that provides easy access to the island's rich culture, gorgeous scenery, and exciting nightlife is the Ibiza Airport (Aeroport d'Eivissa).

Airport in Ibiza: A Doorway to Paradise

Ibiza Airport is a contemporary facility that is positioned on the island's southern shore and built to handle the influx and outflow of visitors interested in the island's varied attractions. It finds a balance between comfort and efficiency with one terminal and a wide range of services.

International Links: Ibiza Airport is a major entrance point for travelers from Europe and other continents, with a vast network of links worldwide. With direct flights available from major destinations including London, Paris, Madrid, and Amsterdam, a diverse spectrum of international passengers can be assured of accessibility. During the summer, when the island sees a spike in tourism, this accessibility is particularly noticeable.

Seasonal Flights: Although flights to Ibiza are available all year round, there is a surge in activity during the summer months as carriers increase their schedules in response to increased demand. Flights are arriving in large numbers to accommodate people who want to enjoy the island's famous nightlife, gorgeous beaches, and exciting cultural activities.

Domestic Connections: Ibiza Airport serves as a domestic gateway for both locals and Spanish nationals visiting the island who want to experience its charms. It connects the island to other parts of Spain. For those looking for a short getaway, convenient access is guaranteed by frequent flights to and from destinations like Barcelona, Madrid, and Valencia.

Airport Facilities: Ibiza Airport offers a number of facilities to improve the quality of your trip. A variety of goods and delectable foods are available at duty-free shops, boutiques, and restaurants. With so many car rental companies to choose from, exploring the island on your own is easy.

Transportation to City Center: There is easy transportation from the airport to Ibiza Town and other locations. Direct access to multiple locations on the island is provided by taxis and private shuttles that are waiting outside the terminal. Regular bus routes also link the airport to well-known locations, giving passengers a cheap choice.

Ibiza Airport sets the standard for the island's friendly hospitality and well-run infrastructure since it serves as many visitors' first point of contact. It's more than just a doorway—rather, it's an introduction to the magical adventures that await on this Mediterranean treasure. Ibiza Airport makes sure the trip is just as unforgettable as the destination itself, whether you're traveling to enjoy calm tranquility, vibrant nightlife, or beaches bathed in sunlight.

Watercraft and Ferries

The seaside charm of Ibiza reaches well beyond its beaches kissed by sunlight. Travelers are welcome to explore the island's hidden coves, nearby isles, and lively coastal settlements thanks to its vast network of ferries and boats. Using the sea to access quiet beaches, go island hopping, or take leisurely cruises is an essential element of visiting Ibiza.

Transportation via Ferry: Entryway to Adjacent Islands

Ferry services are available for adventurous exploration on the waterways between Ibiza and the nearby Balearic islands. The most important of these links is the one that leads to Formentera, a peaceful haven renowned for its immaculate beaches and crystal-clear waters. In less than an hour, regular boats can cover the distance, making them ideal for day getaways or longer island hopping excursions.

Mainland routes Portugal:

Important links to the Spanish mainland are also maintained by Ibiza. Mediterranean ferries provide a picturesque journey from ports such as Valencia, Barcelona, and Denia. With its expansive coastline views and the allure of Ibiza's lively atmosphere just beyond the horizon, the ride itself turns into an enthralling experience.

Customized Journeys with Water Taxis

Water taxis provide a customized kind of maritime transportation for a more personal experience. These agile boats can take you anywhere on the coast of Ibiza whenever you choose. When looking for a private charter, an elite beach club, or a quiet cove, water taxis provide personalized service and flexibility.

Luxury on the High Seas with Charter Services

Renting a private yacht or boat offers an unmatched experience for those looking for the pinnacle of nautical luxury. A variety of boats with professional crews to guarantee a smooth and luxurious journey are available for hiring, including stylish motor yachts and vintage sailboats. With this option, you can go sailing around the untamed coastline and discover hidden harbors.

Sunset Tours and Cruises: Scenery Glimmer

A romantic and unique way to see Ibiza's natural beauty is through sunset cruises. When these guided trips depart in the late afternoon, visitors can see the island's shoreline illuminated by the warm tones of the lowering sun. It's an encounter that, more often than not, captures the enchantment of the landscapes of Ibiza.

The nautical options available in Ibiza offer a gateway to a world of discovery and adventure, whether you choose to take a leisurely ferry ride, hire a private yacht, or use a water taxi to discover hidden coves. Travelers are encouraged to carve out their own route across the glistening waters on each journey, uncovering the special qualities that set this Mediterranean gem apart.

Chapter 3: Allowances

Properties in Ibiza

Ibiza has a wide range of lodging options to suit any traveler's preferences and price range. There are plenty of alternatives on the island, ranging from opulent beachfront resorts and stylish boutique hotels to quaint villas and affordable hostels. Popular hotspots with distinct ambiances include Santa Eulalia, San Antonio, and Ibiza Town. Coastal cities provide picturesque beachfront retreats, while the countryside offers rustic agroturismos for a more peaceful getaway. Amid its sun-kissed surroundings, Ibiza guarantees that every guest finds their perfect escape with options ranging from extravagant to intimate.

Resorts and Hotels

In Ibiza, Hotels & Resorts: Where Comfort and Luxury Come Together
A variety of hotels and resorts that serve discriminating guests looking for an exceptional island experience make up Ibiza's hospitality scene, which is a tapestry of luxury and comfort.
opulent getaways: splendor by the sea

Ibiza is home to an array of luxurious hotels and resorts that are world-class and provide an opulent respite from everyday life. These lodging options are the definition of luxury, ranging from well-known coastal properties to exclusive mountaintop retreats. Throughout their stay, guests can expect to be pampered in an opulent cocoon thanks to suites featuring private patios, infinity pools with views of the Mediterranean, and personalized concierge services.

Boutique Elegance: Cozy and Elegant
Ibiza's boutique hotels are full of personality and charm; they are frequently located in quaint rural communities or exquisitely restored ancient houses. These small businesses place a high value on individualized service while offering a distinctive and intimate experience to their visitors. An atmosphere of understated elegance is created by elegantly designed rooms, locally inspired decor, and a focus on local cuisine.

Resorts that are Family-Friendly: All Ages
Families looking for an amazing holiday can find refuge in Ibiza, in addition to being a popular location for partygoers. A variety of amenities catered to the needs of adults and children can be found in family-friendly resorts. Everyone can enjoy the island's splendor, from the youngest to the oldest, thanks to kid's clubs, family suites, and activities like mini-golf, water sports, and nature tours.

Wellness Getaways: Harmonizing Mind, Body, and Soul

Ibiza is now known as a centre for holistic living and wellbeing. Spa services, yoga retreats, and wellness programs designed to revitalize the mind, body, and soul are available in well-being resorts. For those looking to relax and rediscover balance, these secluded havens within the island's scenic surroundings offer a peaceful haven.

Sea Views and Serenity Abound in Beachfront Bliss

With their prime locations along the coast, several hotels and resorts in Ibiza provide easy access to the breathtaking beaches of the island. Only a short distance from their lodging, visitors can enjoy the tranquil murmur of the waves and the warm embrace of the sun. The experience is completed by dining establishments and bars along the beach, which offer a perfect atmosphere for celebration and relaxation.

Ibiza's lodging options are a major part of the island's appeal, ranging from opulent resorts that redefine luxury to smaller hotels that radiate personality and charm. Each place has an own story to tell, providing visitors with an experience that enhances the beauty and liveliness of this Mediterranean treasure. Ibiza's hotels and resorts are prepared to surpass expectations and produce priceless experiences, whether you're looking for a quiet getaway or a vibrant beach getaway.

Holiday Homes and Villas

Villas and Holiday Homes: Customized Getaways in Ibiza

Ibiza villas and vacation rentals provide a home away from home for those looking for a more individualized and private getaway, with the added attraction of the island's breathtaking scenery and lively culture.

Quiet Spots: Seclusion in Heaven

Each Ibiza villa offers a private haven for visitors to relax and take in the island's natural splendor, from opulent beachfront estates to quaint rural hideaways. These villas provide an unmatched amount of solitude and peace, along with large living areas, private pools, and lush gardens.

Customized Experiences with Adaptable Choices

There are many options available in Ibiza vacation rentals to meet the needs of any kind of traveler. Whether you're looking for a vast estate for a particular event, a family-friendly villa with many bedrooms, or a romantic one-bedroom cottage, there is a wide range of properties to pick from. It is up to the guests to personalize their stay in order to suit their tastes.

Authentic Experiences with a Local Charm

Ibiza's distinctive character is reflected in the architecture and design of many of the villas and holiday rentals there. With contemporary conveniences added, traditional fincas (farmhouses) have been painstakingly refurbished to retain their original character. Others include modern buildings that easily mix in with the surrounding landscape.

Facilities and Offerings: Deluxe Living

A wide range of amenities are included in Ibiza villas and vacation rentals to improve the visitor experience. A welcoming atmosphere is created by large living rooms, fully furnished kitchens, and outdoor entertaining areas. To further enhance the experience, extra services can be scheduled, such as personal chefs, housekeeping, and concierge support.

Perfect for Celebrations & Groups: Entertaining in Style

These lodging options are especially ideal for special events and group trips. Villas and holiday rentals give you the room and freedom to host events in elegance, whether it's a group retreat, a destination wedding, or a family reunion. Enormous outdoor spaces and services for event coordination guarantee that no detail is overlooked.

Local Views: Dedicated Concierge

Ibiza is home to a large number of villa and vacation rental companies that offer individualized concierge services and insider knowledge of the best places to visit. These businesses make sure visitors get the most out of their time on the island by organizing excursions and activities and making restaurant recommendations.

A private and customized method to take in the beauty and culture of the island is offered by Ibiza villas and holiday rentals. These lodgings provide a platform from which to explore the beauty of Ibiza, crafting treasured experiences that last a lifetime, with a variety of options to suit varying tastes and group sizes.

Cost-effective Choices

Low-Cost Options: Reasonably Priced Getaways in Ibiza

Known for its opulent offers, Ibiza welcomes visitors on a tight budget as well. For those looking for an inexpensive but unforgettable trip, the island offers a wide range of lodging, entertainment, and food choices.

Budget-Friendly Lodging: Hostels and Guesthouses

Hostels and guesthouses are among the affordable lodging options available in Ibiza. These places offer tidy, pleasant rooms at affordable prices. They provide a useful and reasonably priced base for visiting the island, even though they do not have the extravagance of upscale resorts.

Apartments for Self-Catering: Flexibility and Economical

An affordable substitute for regular hotels in Ibiza is to rent a self-catering apartment. Because these apartments have kitchens, visitors may make their food and reduce their eating costs. They also provide the freedom to customize the stay to fit different needs and budgets.

Local Restaurants: Real Tastes at Affordable Prices

The cuisine of Ibiza suits every budget. Local restaurants, sometimes called "menu del día" places, have reasonably priced fixed-price menus with a selection of traditional meals. Savoring genuine Ibicencan delicacies without going over budget is possible with these hidden treasures.

Public Transport: Economical Mode of Mobility

The affordable way to see the island is by making use of Ibiza's well-functioning public transit system. At fair prices, buses connect major towns, beaches, and tourist destinations. It's a sensible option for tourists on a tight budget because multi-journey passes may be purchased for additional discounts.

Nature and Culture: Free or Cheap Activities

Immersion in the island's natural beauty and cultural legacy is made possible by the abundance of free or inexpensive activities that Ibiza has to offer. Hiking along coastal trails, spending a day at one of the many public beaches on the island, or exploring the historic alleys of Ibiza Town's Dalt Vila are all worthwhile activities that can be done for little to no money.

Seasonal Savings on Off-Peak Travel

Savings can be substantial when you travel in the shoulder seasons, which are usually spring and fall. There is less crowding at major sights and accommodation prices are generally lower. Travelers on a tight budget should take advantage of the lovely weather that is still around.

With its wide range of offerings, Ibiza serves budget-conscious tourists who don't want to sacrifice pleasure for price. Budget-conscious travelers can experience Ibiza's allure and make priceless memories without breaking the bank by choosing affordable lodging, dining at local eateries, or touring the island's scenic landscapes.

Chapter 4: Ibiza's Best Beaches

Top Beaches in Ibiza

The coastline of Ibiza reveals a mosaic of gorgeous beaches, each with its charms. A perennial favorite is Cala Comte, with its pristine seas and breathtaking sunsets. Ses Salines enchants with its unspoiled beauty and lively ambiance, while Playa d'en Bossa calls with its bright clubs and white sands. Benirràs Beach, with its pristine waters, is a tranquil haven tucked away among striking rocks. These beaches, along with many more, highlight the varied coastal grandeur of Ibiza and invite both nature lovers and sun worshippers to enjoy the island's unparalleled natural beauty.

The Comte de Cala

Cala Comte: A Gem in the Mediterranean
Tucked away along the western shore of Ibiza, Cala Comte is a genuine gem of the Mediterranean. This charming cove charms guests with its unspoiled beauty and tranquil atmosphere. It is well-known for its transparent seas and stunning sunsets.

Golden sands and turquoise waters:

Cala Comte is well-known for its crystal clear, turquoise-colored waves that softly caress the fine, golden dunes. It's a great place to swim and snorkel because of the shallow depths, which let tourists see the colorful marine life that resides in the quiet, clear water.

Magnificent views of the setting sun

Cala Comte displays a captivating show of hues as the day draws to an end. A warm warmth is projected across the ocean as the horizon changes into a tapestry of blazing reds and oranges. One of the island's most beloved views is this magnificent sunset, which draws both tourists and residents to see nature's nightly masterpiece.

Beach Clubs and Amenities: To improve the quality of the guest experience, Cala Comte provides a variety of amenities. Mediterranean food, crisp cocktails, and relaxed music are served at the beach clubs and eateries that border the shore. Rentable sunbeds and umbrellas provide for a relaxing and comfortable beach day.

Stunning Views of Illa des Bosc: Illa des Bosc is a small rocky islet located off the coast of Cala Comte. This deserted island gives the beach a captivating backdrop and enhances the picturesque surroundings with a panorama of natural beauty.

Vibrant Atmosphere and Diverse Crowd: The allure of Cala Comte is felt by a wide range of travelers. The friendly atmosphere of the beach attracts families, couples, and single visitors. The beach is the perfect place for people looking for leisure activities and relaxation because of its accessibility and variety of attractions.

Hiking and Nature Trails: Cala Comte provides access to neighboring hiking trails for individuals who enjoy exploring. Nature lovers can explore the island's natural splendor on foot thanks to the craggy shoreline and picturesque cliffs.

Accessibility & Nearby San Antonio: Cala Comte is easily accessible due to its close vicinity to the municipality of San Antonio. Visitors can experience this adjacent hub's busy nightlife, food options, and cultural activities with a short drive or a leisurely walk along the coast.

Ibiza's captivating coastline charm is exemplified by Cala Comte, a place of unmatched natural beauty and serene ambiance. This Mediterranean jewel invites guests to lose themselves in its timeless splendor, whether they're there for an evening of breathtaking sunsets or a day of sun-soaked leisure.

The Bossa Beach

Ibiza's coastline revolves around Playa d'en Bossa.

Playa d'en Bossa, a vibrant seaside community that stretches along Ibiza's southeast coast, is bustling with activity both during the day and at night. This energetic beach location is well-known for its fine sands, energetic ambiance, and variety of internationally recognized beach clubs and nightlife establishments.

Beach Bliss: Azure waters and golden sands

The lovely golden sands at Playa d'en Bossa extend out generously and slope softly into the bright blue seas of the Mediterranean. Families and swimmers find it to be a welcoming location due to its shallow depths, while those who enjoy water sports can engage in jet skiing and paddleboarding, among other activities.

Famous Beach Clubs: A Symbolic Experience

Some of the world's most prestigious beach clubs can be found in Playa d'en Bossa. Famous pool parties and exciting DJ lineups are often associated with venues such as Ushuaïa and Hi Ibiza. These venues turn the beach into a large dance floor where partygoers dance beneath the stars or the sun, defining the iconic nightlife of Ibiza.

A Tapestry of Cooking: From fine dining to chemicals

Playa d'en Bossa's beachside promenade is lined with a variety of restaurants to suit every taste and budget. While chic beachside restaurants provide a fusion of Mediterranean and international cuisine, chiringuitos (beach bars) serve up fresh fish and tapas. Playa d'en Bossa provides a varied gastronomic adventure, whether you're looking for a laid-back lunch with your toes in the sand or an upscale dining experience.

Beaches Are Not the Only Things to Do and See During the Day

Playa den Bossa has a variety of daytime activities in addition to its lively nightlife and beach. There's no shortage of entertainment options, including beach volleyball courts, boutique stores, and water activity rentals. In addition, there are chances for adventure and relaxation at neighboring attractions like the Aguamar water park, boat trips, and yoga sessions.

Close to Ibiza Town: Blending Seaside and Urban Ecology

The modern capital of Ibiza Island, Playa d'en Bossa, is easily accessible from it. Access to the town's historic area, stylish stores, vibrant bars, and top-notch restaurants can be had with a quick drive or a stroll down the promenade. Because of this proximity, guests may take advantage of the best of both worlds: a calm beach getaway and a lively downtown life.

Playa d'en Bossa is a testament to Ibiza's varied charm, offering a dynamic blend of seaside pleasure, vibrant nightlife, and a diverse selection of activities. Every tourist to Playa den Bossa departs with unforgettable memories, whether they are looking for an exhilarating day of water sports, a night of dancing, or just a day spent lounging in the Mediterranean heat.

Saline Session

A Natural Gem on the Southern Shore of Ibiza, Ses Salines

Ses Salines, an idyllic seaside town on Ibiza's southernmost tip, is well known for its clean beaches, lively atmosphere, and ecological significance. Named for its ancient salt flats, this distinctive area offers travelers a wonderful fusion of the natural world's splendor and vibrant coastal charm.

A Historic Legacy of Salt Flats and Natural Heritage

The term "Ses Salines" refers to the area's former status as a major salt-producing hub. The island's economic and cultural legacy has been shaped by the centuries-long use of salt flats for the extraction of sea salt. These apartments now serve as a reminder of the opulent past of Ibiza.

Pure Beaches and glistening Waters: Seaside Majesty

Several of Ibiza's most recognizable beaches are found in Ses Salines. The kilometer-long stretch of shoreline features pristine white sands and enticingly clear waters. These beaches offer a breathtaking setting for leisure and water-based sports, encircled by aromatic pine forests and craggy cliffs.

Lively Ambiance of Beach Clubs and Chiringuitos

A variety of beach clubs and chiringuitos (beach bars) can be found along the shore, giving Ses Salines an energetic beach vibe. These places provide a fusion of cuisine, music, and beachside leisure. Ses Salines captures the essence of the Ibiza experience, offering everything from yoga classes at dawn to sunset cocktails.

Ses Salines Natural Park: A Biodiversity Refuge

Biodiversity is protected at the Ses Salines Natural Park, a land- and sea-based protected area. The rich diversity of flora and fauna is supported by diverse ecosystems, such as dunes, salt pans, and wetlands. It is an important ecological zone because migratory birds and endangered animals use this pristine area as a haven.

Nature Trails & Hiking: Discovering the Wild Side

Hiking trails crisscross the steep landscape of Ses Salines, inviting nature enthusiasts to explore. With their spectacular panoramic views of the Mediterranean, these trails wind through pine forests, salt flats, and coastal cliffs. It is a chance to establish a more profound connection with the island's natural beauty.

Gastronomic Adventures with Culinary Delights and Local Fare

The exceptional culinary options in the Ses Salines region are well-known. Seafood and Mediterranean dishes are served in a delicious variety at restaurants and chiringuitos. A delectable sample of the island's culinary legacy is offered by freshly caught seafood, regional products, and traditional Ibicencan meals.

Ses Salines perfectly captures the essence of the southern coast of Ibiza, combining natural beauty, cultural value, and a lively seaside vibe. Visitors to Ses Salines are rewarded with an experience that embodies the island's enduring charm, whether they choose to explore the salt flats, lounge on immaculate beaches, or indulge in delectable cuisine.

The Benirràs Cove

Beach Benirràs: A Calm Haven Below the Cliffs in Ibiza

Benirràs Beach is a peaceful, serene refuge of natural beauty nestled along Ibiza's northwest shore. The pristine waters and peaceful atmosphere of this charming cove, which is bordered by old pine trees and framed by rocky cliffs, enthrall tourists.

Enchanted Scene: The Masterwork of Nature

Benirràs is surrounded by stunning cliffs, which form a remote cove that resembles a well-kept secret. Soft sand and sleek pebbles decorate the shoreline, luring tourists to unwind and enjoy the sunshine. It's a great place to swim and snorkel because of the calm waves and shallow seas.

Hippie Legacy: An Unconventional Legacy

Ibiza's countercultural past is preserved at Benirràs Beach. During the 1960s and 1970s, it developed into a meeting spot for musicians, artists, and free spirits. Drum circles, vibrant stalls, and a noticeable bohemian vibe that permeates the beach are all evidence of this era's legacy.

Rituals of the Sunset: An Enthralling Display

The magnificent sunsets of Benirràs are well known. The horizon becomes a canvas of bright colors and purples as the day comes to an end, illuminating the sea with a warm glow. On Sunday nights, local musicians get together to create a captivating soundtrack for the lowering sun, making these evenings especially memorable.

Rocky Sentinel Illa des Bosc

The rocky islet of Illa des Bosc is located off the coast of Benirràs. This deserted island with pine trees growing out of it gives the beach a charming backdrop. It offers a chance to explore a beautiful natural refuge and is a popular destination for daring swimmers and kayakers.

Gourmet Treats: Seaside Restaurant

There are several chiringuitos and quaint beachside eateries on Benirràs Beach. Many Mediterranean and regional cuisines, frequently with a focus on recently caught fish, are offered at these restaurants. A genuinely magical culinary experience may be had when dining on the beach with the sound of the waves playing in the background.

Hiking & Nature Trails: Exploring the Beauty of the Environment

Benirràs provides access to picturesque hiking routes for those who can't wait to explore beyond the shore. Trails meander through pine forests and beside coastal bluffs, offering breathtaking views of the Mediterranean.

Walking the island's natural splendor is a great way to experience it.

Visitors are invited to absorb the spirit of Ibiza's natural splendor by Benirràs Beach, which boasts a calm atmosphere and rough beauty. This Mediterranean treasure delivers an experience that makes a lasting impression on every visitor, whether they choose to relax on its pebbled sands, explore the coastline, or take in a breathtaking sunset.

Chapter 5: After-Dark Activities & Amusement

Ibiza's Entertainment and Nightlife

Renowned for its vibrant nightlife, Ibiza attracts partygoers from all over the world. After dark, the island comes alive with excitement and offers a wide range of places and events. Top DJs create an exhilarating atmosphere at world-class clubs like Pacha, Amnesia, and Privilege. As the sun sets, beach clubs become lively dance floors instead of serene havens. More personal settings can be found in Ibiza Town and San Antonio at little bars and live music venues. Ibiza's nightlife culture delivers an unmatched blend of music, dancing, and exciting social events that redefine the very essence of midnight celebration, from open-air parties to stylish rooftop lounges.

Pubs & Clubs

Clubs and Bars: Ibiza's Center of Nightlife

Ibiza's legendary clubs and bars serve as the foundation for its image as the heart of electronic music and lively nightlife worldwide. A mosaic of nighttime entertainment that has come to symbolize the island's personality is created by the distinct experiences that each location delivers.

famous clubs: the heart of the nightlife

The biggest stars in the electronic music industry have played at Ibiza's clubs, which have gained international recognition. Pacha radiates refinement and glitz with its recognizable cherry logo. Amnesia's massive dance floors and vivid light displays produce a thrilling environment. The largest nightclub in the world, Privilege, is renowned for its expansive rooms. Ibiza is known for being the best place for lovers of electronic music, and these venues contribute to that reputation.

Dancing Under the Stars at Open-Air Extravaganzas

The outdoor nightlife scene in Ibiza offers a distinctive experience that combines music with the stunning scenery of the island. With its star-studded line-ups and poolside events, Ushuaïa Beach Club turns into a vibrant dance floor when the sun sets. Situated amidst fig trees, DC-10 is highly regarded for its underground sounds and cozy atmosphere. These locations create a one-of-a-kind sensory experience by skillfully fusing music, nature, and celebration.

Elegant Beach Clubs: Rhythms by the Sea Ibiza's beach clubs redefine coastal leisure, fusing daytime calm with late-night partying. Beachfront parties, fine cuisine, and sun-drenched leisure may be found in upscale settings at places like Blue Marlin and Nikki Beach. These locations become chic gathering places for dancing, music, and cocktails as the day turns into night, all against the backdrop of the Mediterranean.

Intimate Social Retreats: Bohemian Bars

Ibiza has a reputation for having very energetic clubs, but it also has a lot of little bars with a bohemian vibe. For those looking for a more laid-back option, Ibiza Town's cobblestone alleys are home to a variety of unique establishments like La Bodega and Bar Costa. These places, which offer a break from the throbbing energy of the clubs, are characterized by live music, locally produced art, and a friendly atmosphere.

A Toast to the Beauty of Nature at Sunset Bars

Famous for its sunsets, Ibiza offers front-row seats to this nightly sight from several bars along the coast. Renowned locations such as Café del Mar, Café Mambo, and Savannah are where people congregate to watch the sunset while enjoying well-chosen music and delicious beverages.

The clubs and bars of Ibiza are more than just places to go; they are an essential component of the island's culture, a meeting place for music, the outdoors, and a variety of social encounters. Ibiza offers a wide variety of nightlife options to suit every taste and preference, making the celebrations as exciting and varied as the island itself. Some of these options include the throbbing beats of a world-class DJ, a serene sunset toast, or the cozy companionship of a boho bar.

Vacation Get-Aways

Beach Parties: Dance Under the Stars at Ibiza's Iconic Event

The shores that round this Mediterranean gem are resonant with Ibiza's magnetic charm, which reaches far beyond its clubs. Beach parties, a mainstay of the island's nightlife, provide a unique and immersive experience where sand, music, and water come together to create magical moments.

Nature's Dance Floor: Shoreline Beats

Ibiza is known for its ability to effortlessly blend throbbing sounds with natural beauty, as evidenced by its beach parties. Under a starry sky, these parties take place on the smooth dunes, with the soothing sound of breaking waves creating a mesmerizing background. A vibrant mood envelops the revelers as the vast shoreline is transformed into a dance floor.

Magic in the Dusk: Sunset Sessions

As the sun sets, the beaches of Ibiza are bathed in an ethereal glow that sets the stage for the evening's festivities. Beach gatherings frequently begin in the late afternoon, giving guests a chance to take in the renowned sunsets on the island. The music gets louder as the sky bursts into a spectrum of flaming colors, creating an unearthly sensation that stays with you.

renowned beach locations: legends in the sand

Famous locations along the coast of Ibiza offer beach parties. Resorts with carefully chosen lineups and beautiful surroundings include Sands Ibiza in Playa d'en Bossa and Amante Beach Club in Sol d'en Serra. Ibiza's beach party culture is embodied by these locations, which combine natural beauty with elite DJ sets.

Different Tone of Music: From Mellow to Intensive

Ibiza beach parties offer a wide range of musical preferences. Some gatherings include music that is relaxed and breezy so that guests can lounge and enjoy the atmosphere. Others develop into exuberant dance events where DJs spin electronic, techno, and house sounds that echo throughout the evening and entice guests to let go of their inhibitions and grooves.

Drum Circles and Fire Performances: A Bohemian Spirit

Ibiza's beach parties continue to embody the bohemian attitude that characterized the island's early counterculture. The celebrations are given a dash of spontaneity with drum circles, fire shows, and unscheduled jam sessions. These natural components create a sense of community celebration by allowing guests to take part in the experience's production.

Being inclusive and accessible: A World Convocation

The inclusiveness of beach parties in Ibiza is widely recognized. A global community brought together by a love of music and the allure of Ibiza's shoreline, visitors from all over the world congregate on the island's coasts. Every beach party is a special and remarkable event because of the varied groups of people who contribute to the rich tapestry of experiences.

Beach parties in Ibiza are evidence of the island's capacity to produce transcendental experiences. These get-togethers celebrate life, love, and the enchantment that is exclusively Ibiza, with nature serving as the backdrop, music serving as the medium, and a diverse worldwide community serving as the attendees.

Events for Music

Ibiza Music Festivals: A Place Where Bliss Meets Beats

Unquestionably the center of the world for electronic music, Ibiza presents an incredible selection of music festivals that bring people from all over the world. These immersive events are not like traditional concerts; instead, they create a communal experience in which culture, music, and environment converge into a crescendo of celebration and rhythm.

The International Meeting of Electronic Music Minds, or IMS Ibiza

For those working in the electronic music industry, the International Music Summit (IMS) in Ibiza serves as a guide. This yearly gathering brings together musicians, thinkers, and fans of the genre to talk, argue, and create the genre's future. Panels, workshops, and showcases make IMS Ibiza, a bustling center for networking, information exchange, and honoring the craft of electronic music.

House music extravaganza at the Defected Ibiza Festival

The Defected Ibiza Festival is a dynamic celebration of dance music that takes place at various locations throughout the island. Ibiza's famous venues are transformed into vivid dance floors for this festival, which is renowned for its thrilling DJ lineups and irresistible tunes. The festival captures the essence of house music culture, with venues ranging from famous clubs like Amnesia to beach clubs.

UNESCO Heritage Site Dalt Vila as a Stage

Some of the most prominent music events on the island take place against the breathtaking backdrop of Ibiza Town's ancient area, Dalt Vila. Internationally renowned musicians perform on the historic walls of this UNESCO World Heritage Site, fusing the vibrant music scene of the island with its rich past. The experience is bizarre and unforgettable because of the juxtaposition of modern beats and historic walls.

IMS Dalt Vila: A Glorious Evening of Electronic Music

The IMS Held inside Ibiza Town's medieval walls, Dalt Vila is an annual event. In a stunning display of aural brilliance, this outdoor extravaganza brings together pioneers of electronic music with up-and-coming talent. Attendees are in for an unmatched musical immersion experience set against the backdrop of Dalt Vila's historic stone ramparts and expansive vistas of the Mediterranean.

Amante Beach Club: A Fusion of Music and Nature

Embracing the natural beauty of its surroundings, exclusive music concerts take place at Amante Beach Club, tucked amid the cliffs of Sol d'en Serra. Renowned for its breathtaking views of the sea, this venue creates a cozy atmosphere for DJ sets and live music events. Amante Beach Club is a favorite hangout for music lovers because of its unique blend of nature, music, and Mediterranean charm.

Past Beats: Intercultural Communication and Community

Music festivals in Ibiza are more than just entertainment; they serve as engines for cross-cultural dialogue and communal development. People come to the island from all walks of life and bond with each other via their passion for music. It's a chance to embrace the uniqueness and the communal spirit that characterizes Ibiza's music scene.

Music festivals in Ibiza are more than just gatherings; they're immersive experiences that honor the core values of electronic music culture. The island's varied landscapes are transformed into stages where beats echo during these festivals, which take place on sun-kissed beaches and medieval fortresses. The result is moments of sheer transcendence that stay in memory long after the music ends.

Chapter 6. Food and Dining

Ibiza Cuisine & Dining: A Gastronomic Odyssey
Ibiza offers a delicious blend of Mediterranean cuisine and international influences in its culinary scene. The island's culinary scene offers something for every taste, from creative fusion cuisine to classic Spanish tapas. Ibiza's gastronomy is characterized by its use of fresh fish, locally grown products, and fragrant herbs. Upscale restaurants serve gourmet cuisine, while beachside chiringuitos serve informal fare while you dip your toes in the sand. The food scene in Ibiza is as varied as its guests, so every meal is an unforgettable taste adventure and a celebration of the island's rich culinary legacy.

Regional Distinctives

Ibiza's Culinary Treasures are the local specialty.
The rich cultural legacy of the island is reflected in the diverse flavors and traditional delights found in Ibiza's culinary environment. Ibiza's regional specialties provide a fascinating tour through its culinary heritage, ranging from fresh fish to hearty stews.

Bullit de Peix: A Seafood-Inspired Pleasure
The traditional Ibicencan meal bullit de peix honors the island's abundant marine life. This fragrant fish stew is

made with potatoes, aromatic saffron, and locally caught fish, usually grouper or rockfish. The traditional accompaniment to the dish is alioli, a garlicky sauce made with mayonnaise that provides a creamy counterpoint to the strong tastes of the stew.

Sofrit Pagès: A Fond Island Banquet
In honor of Ibiza's agricultural heritage, Sofrit Pagès is a filling and rustic dish. This aromatic stew is made with a variety of slow-cooked meats, such as chicken, lamb, and sobrasada, a hot cured sausage, together with seasonal vegetables. The recipe has a rich flavor thanks to the powerful spices and fragrant herbs, making it a hearty and filling supper.

Peix Sec: A Heritage of Cuisine
A longstanding mainstay of Ibiza cuisine is peix sec or dried fish. In the past, fish like bonito or Dorada were salted and allowed to air dry, giving the islanders a preserved food source. Peix Sec is now widely enjoyed in contemporary forms, frequently offered as a tapa or in salads, giving guests a taste of Ibiza's rich culinary history.

Greixonera: A Delicious Comfort Food
A delicious delicacy that perfectly captures the richness of Ibiza's culinary heritage is called greixonera. Local ensaimada pastry, soaked in milk, eggs, and sugar and

enhanced with aromatic cinnamon and lemon zest, is the centerpiece of this baked custard dessert. Greixonera is a rich and satisfying dish that, when served warm, gives a taste of the island's aromatic and sweet side.

Ibicencas Hierbas: A Herbal Concoction
A classic liqueur called Hierbas Ibicencas embodies the essence of the fragrant plants of Ibiza. This beloved elixir is a treasured part of the island's culinary legacy. It is made from a blend of indigenous herbs, including rosemary, thyme, and fennel, infused in alcohol with an anise flavor. It provides a glass of Ibiza's natural abundance and is frequently savored as a digestif.

A gastronomic voyage through the history, culture, and natural riches of Ibiza can be had by sampling the local specialties. Every meal is a celebration of the island's diverse culinary heritage, with dishes ranging from robust stews to sweet delights that each reflect the many flavors and traditions that constitute Ibiza's rich gastronomic tapestry.

Elegant Eating

Ibiza's Fine Dining: Mediterranean Epicurean Excellence
The food culture in Ibiza is more sophisticated than its typical offerings, showcasing the island's inventiveness and inventiveness in the kitchen. Fine dining places in

Ibiza provide a masterful blend of regional ingredients and worldwide influences, resulting in a symphony of flavors that turn dining into a work of art.

Star-Studded Magnificence: Ibiza's Culinary Stars

Ibiza is home to a plethora of Michelin-starred eateries that are shining examples of fine dining. Reputable restaurants with coveted Michelin awards include Restaurante Es Trull de Can Palau, which is noted for its imaginative Mediterranean meals, and El Portalon, which is well-known for its inventive Spanish cuisine. These restaurants are redefining the island's culinary scene with their well-prepared food, which is a showcase for culinary expertise.

Creative Works of Art: Combination of Local and Global

Ibiza's fine dining is defined by a tasteful blend of global methods and regional ingredients. Prominent culinary artists are inspired by the abundance of produce on the island and use seasonal ingredients, flavorful herbs, and fresh fish in their recipes. The end product is a symphony of flavors and sensations that pushes the limits of culinary innovation while honoring Ibiza's rich culinary history.

Sightseeing Pleasures: Magnificent Display and Ambience

In Ibiza, fine dining is a multisensory experience that goes beyond taste. Every meal is a culinary masterpiece, expertly arranged to wow the senses. Restaurants frequently have exquisite settings, complete with chic furnishings and breathtaking views of the Mediterranean that provide the perfect atmosphere for an amazing dining experience.

Wine Pairing Expertise: A Harmony of Tastes

In Ibiza, fine dining places a premium on well-chosen wine pairings. Restaurants have long wine menus that feature worldwide and regional varieties. Sommeliers are experts in guiding patrons through the complexities of wine selection, elevating the flavors of each meal through tasteful pairings that enhance the dining experience.

Tailored Service: Gastronomic Adventures specific to the guests

In Ibiza, excellent service is often associated with fine meals. Restaurants place a high value on providing each customer with individualized attention so that their eating experience is customized to their tastes. A smooth and enjoyable dining experience is created by the attentive waitstaff and expert sommeliers who provide excellent service to match the culinary artistry.

Ibiza's fine dining venues provide an extraordinary culinary journey that highlights the island's culinary prowess. A journey of epicurean exploration that honors the artistry of food and the depth of Ibiza's culinary legacy, these restaurants reinvent the dining experience with their Michelin-starred accolades, inventive concoctions, and steadfast devotion to perfection.

Restaurants by the Beach

Beachfront Dining Establishments: A Fusion of Gourmet Flavors with Coastal Magnificence
The dining experience at Ibiza's beachside restaurants skillfully combines the island's rich culinary legacy with its scenic surroundings. Nestled along the coast, these businesses provide a delicious selection of cuisine that highlights the wealth of land and sea, all while providing a front-row seat to the Mediterranean's beautiful landscapes.
With your toes in the sand, enjoy a panoramic meal.
With their feet tucked into soft sand and the soothing sound of waves as their soundtrack, beachfront restaurants in Ibiza provide an unmatched eating experience. The expansive vistas of the Mediterranean, particularly at dusk, provide a mesmerizing atmosphere that enhances the taste experience.
An Extravaganza of Fresh Seafood: From Ocean to Plate
Ibiza's beachside gastronomy is known for its emphasis on locally sourced, fresh fish. Chefs create a wide variety of delicacies that highlight the Mediterranean's rich aquatic life. These eateries provide elaborate seafood paellas and luscious grilled fish, among other

delectable dishes that highlight the island's abundant marine resources.

Mediterranean Cooking: Honoring Regional Products

Ibiza's thriving agricultural past serves as inspiration for beachfront restaurants there. A variety of meals made with locally obtained produce, such as sun-ripened tomatoes, aromatic herbs, and other seasonal ingredients, are frequently found on menus. The dining experience is elevated by this dedication to using high-quality, fresh ingredients, resulting in a true celebration of Mediterranean flavors.

Chiringuitos: Easygoing Beachside Appeal

Beach bars, or chimicitos, are a staple of Ibiza's waterfront restaurant culture. These quaint restaurants invite patrons to unwind and enjoy the tastes of the Mediterranean with an air of ease and casualness. Chiringuitos provide a casual yet delicious dining experience by specializing in grilled seafood, tapas, and refreshing beverages.

Dining at Sunset: An Otherworldly Evening Event

The sunsets in Ibiza are legendary, and dining at beachside restaurants provide a perfect atmosphere to enjoy this nightly show. Diners are treated to a stunning display of colors as the sun sets, adding an extra magical element to the dining experience.

Beachfront Bars for Chill and Cocktails

Ibiza's trendy bars, which provide a variety of unique cocktails and refreshing drinks, are a feature of many seaside eateries. Visitors can unwind with a drink in hand and take in the vibe of the seaside while listening to live music or DJ performances that frequently coincide with the evening.

The island's natural beauty and its thriving culinary culture are combined in the beachside restaurants of Ibiza, providing a gastronomic adventure. These restaurants offer an eating experience that stays in mind long after the meal is finished, making an enduring impression on every guest, whether they are enjoying freshly caught seafood, toasting to a captivating sunset, or just taking in the tranquil coastal setting.

Chapter 7. Activities and Attractions

Activities and Attractions in Ibiza

Ibiza is a treasure trove of experiences, catering to a diverse array of interests. For beach lovers, the island's crystalline shores offer a sun-soaked paradise. History enthusiasts can explore ancient fortresses like Dalt Vila, a UNESCO World Heritage Site. Adventurers can hike scenic trails, while water sports enthusiasts can indulge in everything from snorkeling to jet-skiing. Ibiza's legendary nightlife beckons with world-renowned clubs and beach parties. Additionally, the island's vibrant markets, like Las Dalias, offer a taste of local culture. From cultural landmarks to adrenaline-pumping activities, Ibiza's attractions ensure there's something for everyone to savor and explore.

Sports in Water

Ibiza Water Sports: Adventures in the Sea Hold on
Water sports aficionados have the perfect playground in Ibiza thanks to its blue waters and mild weather. Diverse aquatic activities that suit all skill levels and adrenaline thresholds are available on the island, ranging from tranquil explorations to thrilling thrills.

Kiteboarding and Windsurfing: Taking to the Waves
Ibiza is a windsurfer's dream due to the constant sea breezes and advantageous currents on the island. Famous for their windsurfing courses and equipment rentals, beaches like Playa d'en Bossa and Cala Martina attract both novice and expert surfers. Kitesurfing is a thrilling combination of windsurfing and paragliding that is popular on the coast of Ibiza. It offers thrill-seekers an unforgettable experience.

Under the Surface: Snorkeling and Scuba Diving

A rich underwater environment brimming with marine life and intriguing rock formations can be found along Ibiza's shoreline. You may discover hidden coves, marine caves, and vibrant reefs by going on snorkeling and scuba diving tours. A variety of creatures, including groupers, octopuses, and moray eels, can be seen by divers as they explore the island's fascinating underwater environments.

Adrenaline-Pumped Excitations with Jet Skiing and Watercraft Adventures

Jet skiing down Ibiza's beachfront is an exciting experience for anyone looking for an adrenaline rush. Riding around the island's bays and coves, as well as visiting other islets, is made possible via rental services and guided tours. Paddleboards and speedboats are among the other available watercraft, offering chances for self-directed or guided exploration.

Enjoy Calm Adventures with Paddle Boarding and Kayaking

Kayaking and paddle boarding provide a tranquil substitute for exhilarating water activities. The serene coves and glistening seas of Ibiza provide the perfect environment for leisurely canoeing. A peaceful and personal relationship with the island's coastline beauty can be had by exploring sea caves, canoeing the coast, or visiting isolated beaches.

Parasailing: Gliding Across the Water

Ibiza's breathtaking shoreline can be seen from above when you go parasailing on the island. The thrill-seekers get an amazing experience as they soar through the skies while strapped to a parachute and towed behind a speedboat. From this location, tourists can enjoy expansive views of the Mediterranean including the rocky cliffs and shoreline of Ibiza.

Boat Trips & Yacht Charters: Watery Getaways

A unique way to see the island's splendor is to explore it by boat. Several operators offer guided trips that let visitors explore secret coves, visit nearby islets, and even watch the stunning sunset from the sea. Yacht charters provide an opulent and exclusive getaway with onboard amenities and customized itineraries for a more unique experience.

Immersion in the island's aquatic delights is guaranteed for both adventurers and water aficionados thanks to Ibiza's abundance of water sports opportunities. Ibiza's gorgeous shoreline and crystal-clear waters make you the ideal setting for amazing aquatic excursions, whether you're looking for calm explorations or adrenaline-pumping experiences.

Trails and Natural Areas

Discovering Ibiza's Wild Side through Hiking and Nature Reserves

Hikers and nature lovers will find a rough and wild landscape beyond Ibiza's bustling nightlife and sun-kissed beaches. A haven for wildlife and a canvas for outdoor exploration, the island's varied features include rocky cliffs, pine-covered hills, and immaculate beaches.

Ses Salines Natural Park: A Paradise on the Coast
Nestled on the southern coast of Ibiza, Ses Salines Natural Park is a protected area where beautiful convergences of marine and terrestrial ecosystems can be found. Seagrass meadows, dunes, wetlands, and salt flats combine to provide a diverse range of ecosystems. Along its coasts, endangered species like the loggerhead sea turtle seek protection, as do migratory birds like herons and flamingos.
Ibiza's Highest Peak, Sa Talaia
The tallest peak in Ibiza is Sa Talaia, which rises 475 meters above sea level. This expansive viewpoint, which is found in the island's southwest, provides stunning views of the Mediterranean and the surroundings. Ascending hiking trails go to the summit, offering hikers a view of the entire coast while leading them through aromatic pine trees.
The Mystical Charms of Cala d'Hort Nature Reserve
Cala d'Hort Nature Reserve captures the untamed beauty of Ibiza, nestled on its southwest coast. The famous islets of Es Vedrà and Es Vedranell are surrounded by

towering cliffs that create a mesmerizing effect on the surrounding area. Trekking trails tracing the coastline lead to isolated inlets and vantage points showcasing the captivating interaction of land, sea, and sky.

Es Amunts: North America's Rugged Magnificence

In the northernmost region of Ibiza, Es Amunts reveals a world of wild landscapes and rough beauty. Along the shoreline, this protected area is home to secret coves, fragrant pine trees, and limestone cliffs. Hiking routes allow access to undiscovered gems, such as remote beaches and historic watchtowers, giving visitors a taste of the island's untamed side.

Valley of Santa Agnés: rustic tranquility

Tucked away in the center of Ibiza, the Santa Agnès Valley has a rustic appeal that makes you feel like you're in a different era. This idyllic setting is characterized by terraced fields, almond groves, and ancient whitewashed buildings. The stunning view from the Mirador de Corona is the culmination of a hike across the valley that offers a tranquil immersion in Ibiza's agricultural heritage.

Cami de Cavalls: A Study of the Coast

Hikers can enjoy a lovely route to discover the diverse coastlines of Ibiza along the Cami de Cavalls, often known as the "Horse's Path," which traces the island's shoreline. Offering a panoramic view of Ibiza's stunning coastline, this historic walk meanders through pine forests, past craggy cliffs, and along immaculate beaches.

Ibiza's nature reserves and hiking paths provide access to an unspoiled world of natural beauty and ecological marvels. The island's wild side beckons exploration and discovery, enabling visitors to touch with the timeless spirit of Ibiza's natural splendor. From the protected sanctuaries that harbor various ecosystems to the historic routes that lead travelers over rocky terrain.

Monumental Places

Historical Places: Following the Everlasting Legacy of Ibiza

The rich history of Ibiza is deeply ingrained in the island, creating a tapestry of historic fortifications, amazing archeological finds, and iconic cultural sites. These ancient locations provide insight into the dynamic civilizations that have molded Ibiza's identity by bearing witness to centuries of human presence.

A Living Fortress: Dalt Vila

The fortified ancient town of Ibiza Town, Dalt Vila, is a reminder of the island's legendary past. Impressive walls, cobblestone streets, and a maze-like design that evokes medieval beauty characterize this UNESCO World Heritage Site. Encompassed within are historical gems like the 14th-century Santa Maria Cathedral and the prehistoric Puig des Molins Phoenician necropolis.

Puig de Missa: A Place of Prayer

Puig de Missa is a fascinating collection of architectural and historical marvels that is perched atop a hill in the village of Santa Eulària des Riu. A cemetery, a group of traditional Ibicencan homes, and picturesque viewpoints with expansive views of the island's shore and landscape surround the whitewashed church, which dates back to the 16th century and acts as the focal point.

Tower of Savinar: Keeper of the Coast

Standing guard on the southwest coast of Ibiza is Torre des Savinar, popularly referred to as Pirate's Tower. Perched precariously on a cliff, this 18th-century watchtower was originally used as a lookout to protect against pirate raids. Today, it provides tourists with an amazing view of the mysterious islets of Es Vedranell and Es Vedrà as well as the rocky coastline.

The Phoenician Colony at Sa Caleta: Historic Traces

One of Ibiza's most important archeological sites, Sa Caleta offers a glimpse into the island's Phoenician heritage. This settlement's well-preserved ruins, which date to the 7th century BCE, include circular homes and a protective wall. The location provides priceless insights into the way of life and maritime legacy of the early settlers.

Campanitx Tower: A Watchtower along the Coast

Torre de Campanitx is another of Ibiza's old watchtowers, tucked away on the island's northern coast. Erected in the eighteenth century, it watches over the craggy cliffs and the blue Mediterranean. Ibiza's coastline defense was strengthened by the tower's strategic placement, which enabled it to relay important information to nearby watchtowers.

Cova de Can Marchà: Enchanted Underground Worlds
Hidden deep beneath Port de Sant Miquel's cliffs, Cova de Can Marçà provides an underground exploration of Ibiza's natural and cultural treasures. Beautiful stalactites and stalagmites may be found in this natural cave system, which was originally used by smugglers. The natural beauty of the cave is enhanced by the mystery surrounding its fascinating past, which is told on guided tours.

History comes to life at Ibiza's historical landmarks, which let guests travel back in time and experience the allure of the island's past. A fascinating voyage through time is provided by each site, which ranges from ancient strongholds to archeological wonders and gives witness to the various civilizations that have influenced Ibiza's cultural tapestry.

Purchasing

Ibiza shopping: An eclectic mix of local crafts and bohemian style

The retail environment in Ibiza is a lively blend of artisan markets, bohemian-chic stores, and unique shops. Explore the island's markets to uncover one-of-a-kind gifts; from distinctive fashion finds to handcrafted treasures, the retail scene appeals to a wide range of preferences.

Bohemian Treasures at Hippy Markets

Ibiza's famous hippy markets bear witness to its history as a sanctuary for free spirits and creatives. Perhaps the most well-known, Las Dalias, is a kaleidoscope of vivid energy, live music, and artisan stalls. Visitors can browse a unique selection of handcrafted clothing, jewelry, and international crafts here, all of which are infused with the counterculture legacy of Ibiza.

Boutiques in Ibiza Town: Exquisite Elegance

With its high-end boutiques and designer stores, Ibiza Town gives off an aura of refinement. Renowned fashion names cover the cobblestone lanes of Dalt Vila and the posh avenues of Marina Botafoch, providing a carefully chosen assortment of accessories, beachwear, and haute couture. These shops provide customers looking for a posh and glamorous Ibiza experience.

Craftsmanship: Genuine Ibicencan-Made Items

Genuine Ibicencan mementos are given to guests by local artists who incorporate their traditions into a wide variety of crafts. These works exhibit the hallmarks of traditional craftsmanship, ranging from delicate ceramics to handwoven textiles. Travelers can observe the creative process and purchase one-of-a-kind, locally crafted items at the island's studios and workshops. Mercat Vell: Culinary Delights and Local Flavors

Fresh, locally produced food is the main attraction at Mercat Vell, also known as the Old Market, which is situated in Ibiza Town. A plethora of colorful fruits, fragrant spices, and handcrafted goods fill the stalls, beckoning guests to indulge in the island's culinary abundance. Mercat Vell provides a taste experience of Ibiza's culinary history, ranging from cheeses to olives.

Market Sunday in San Juan: Authentic Charms

Capturing the spirit of rural Ibiza, the San Juan Sunday Market is a bohemian, village-style event. Situated in the quaint village of San Juan, this market offers a variety of products, including organic fruit and handcrafted items. The market's easygoing charm is enhanced by live music and a friendly vibe.

Creative Showcases: Designer Pop-Ups

Pop-up events and designer showcases are two ways that Ibiza's creative spirit is expressed. These vibrant events provide a venue for up-and-coming designers to showcase their works by bringing together talent from across the globe. These events highlight creativity and uniqueness in Ibiza's design scene, encompassing everything from accessories to clothes.

The shopping scene in Ibiza is a celebration of regional craftsmanship and a journey through a tapestry of styles, from high-end glamor to bohemian chic. Visitors are welcome to take part in the lively and diversified retail environment that defines the island's cultural tapestry, whether they choose to browse artisan fairs, stroll down boutique-lined avenues, or find hidden gems in obscure studios.

Chapter 8: Ibiza Town and Old Town (Eivissa)

Ancient Magnificence meets Bright Energy in Ibiza Town and Old Town

The capital of the island, Ibiza Town, combines a seductive old-world charm with contemporary flair. The magnificent Cathedral of Santa Maria towers over the labyrinth of cobblestone lanes, guarded walls, and historic structures that make up Dalt Vila, the Old Town recognized by UNESCO. In between galleries, shops, and bustling plazas, this is where history comes to life. Beyond the walls, upscale eateries, nightclubs, and boutiques line the marina and promenades, which are teeming with urban activity. The vibrant blend of the past and present that is Ibiza Town is where the Mediterranean spirit mingles with modern charm.

Dalt Vila

Dalt Vila: Ibiza's Eternal Palace
The fortified ancient town of Ibiza, known as Dalt Vila, is a living reminder of the island's rich cultural legacy. This UNESCO World Heritage Site is a fascinating maze of cobblestone alleys, old buildings, and historical sites, perched majestically on a hill overlooking Ibiza Town and the Mediterranean Sea.
Historical Relevance: An Array of Ages
The origins of Dalt Vila date back more than 2,500 years, demonstrating the influence of the Roman, Moorish, Phoenician, and Carthaginian civilizations. From the magnificent Portal de ses Taules to the robust ramparts that surround the town, these eras' architectural traces are visible.
The Santa Maria Cathedral: Gothic Elegance
The Cathedral of Santa Maria, a magnificent specimen of Catalan Gothic architecture, is located in the center of Dalt Vila. Over the ages, it underwent extensions and restorations once the building got underway in the 13th century. The cathedral's exquisite craftsmanship and imposing exterior entice people to explore its hallowed chambers, which are home to antiques and artwork dating back hundreds of years.
Time-Stopping Walls in Defensive Architecture
Strong defenses around Dalt Vila were built to protect the town from sea threats. Built mainly in the 16th

century, the walls are an example of 16th-century military engineering. Wandering up the ramparts allows visitors to take in expansive views of the surrounding sea, the harbor, and the town—a viewpoint that has seen centuries of nautical history.

Gallery and Museum Spaces: Preserving the Past Several museums and art galleries in Dalt Vila honor the legendary history of Ibiza. Displaying items spanning millennia, the Archaeological Museum is housed in a mansion built during the Renaissance. In the meantime, modern art venues such as the Puget Museum present a contrast between modern and historical-artistic manifestations.

Artisan shops and boutiques: Mixing the Ancient with the Modern

Boutiques, artisan shops, and galleries can be found throughout Dalt Vila's meandering, small lanes. These businesses provide a carefully chosen assortment of clothing, jewelry, artwork, and crafts that skillfully combine modern inventiveness with the remnants of traditional workmanship.

Squares and Coffee Shops: Calm Havens

The narrow streets of Dalt Vila are broken up by the plazas. The timeless Mediterranean atmosphere of Plaça de Vila is enhanced by its quaint eateries and outdoor dining areas. The quiet area for contemplation that is provided by the cathedral-nested Plaça del Sol is surrounded by the town's old facades.

Dalt Vila is a genuine, breathing example of the ongoing essence of Ibiza, not just a historic enclave. Its historic walls ring with the murmurs of bygone times, beckoning guests to saunter through the pages of history. Dalt Vila is a fundamental part of Ibiza's identity, a location where time stops still and the past and present combine in harmonious beauty, thanks to its breathtaking architecture and lively cultural environment.

Palace of Ibiza

Guardian of the Centuries: Ibiza Castle
Soaring magnificently in the center of Dalt Vila, Ibiza Castle—also referred to as the Castle of Ibiza or Almudaina Castle—is a recognizable symbol of the island's long history. Throughout the ages, this stronghold has withstood numerous marine conquests, cross-cultural interactions, and historical shifts.
Historical Bastion: A Heritage of the Sea
Designed in the twelfth century, under the rule of Alfonso II of Aragon, Ibiza Castle was positioned to fend off maritime attacks. It played a crucial role in defending Ibiza Town and its residents thanks to its strong defenses and prominent position atop the historic Acropolis.
Architectural Importance: A Combination of Styles

The numerous influences that have molded Ibiza's history are reflected in the castle's architectural growth. Built in a straightforward Romanesque style at first, later additions included Baroque, Gothic, and Renaissance architectural elements. With each layer testifying to a distinct period of the island's history, this blending of styles produces an aesthetically striking tapestry.

Guardians of Dalt Vila: A Military Stronghold

The protection of the island against roving pirates and competing maritime powers was greatly aided by Ibiza Castle. Ensuring the safety of the town within, its imposing walls were accompanied by powerful turrets and bastions, acting as a formidable barrier.

Museums and Exhibitions as the Cultural Center

The island's rich history is showcased in museums and cultural exhibitions held at Ibiza Castle these days. The Ibiza Ethnographic Museum, housed inside the castle walls, provides an insight into the customs and way of life of the island's natives. A wide range of contemporary artistic expressions are on display at the Museum of Contemporary Art in the meantime.

Magnificent Views: Aerial and Transverse Views

Views of the town, the harbor, and the glittering Mediterranean Sea are available to guests from the castle's advantageous location atop Dalt Vila. The ongoing fascination of Ibiza's coastline beauty is demonstrated by the stunning vistas that can be seen from the castle ramparts.

Performances and Cultural Events: A Living Monument
Ibiza Castle has developed into a thriving cultural hub that goes beyond its historical function. It holds a variety of events, including musical acts, art exhibits, and theater shows. By bringing vitality to the historic stones, these events guarantee that the castle will always be a vibrant and beloved center for cultural expression.

Ibiza Castle is more than just a stronghold; it is a dynamic example of the island's cultural development and resiliency. Centuries of history, from naval victories to creative expression, are documented within its walls. Ibiza Castle is a cornerstone of Dalt Vila, beckoning guests to experience a trip back in time, meander amid historical echoes, and take in the island citadel's timeless splendor.

Island Chain of Botafoch

Marina Botafoch, Ibiza: Glamour on the Waterfront
Ensconced along the dazzling seashore, Marina Botafoch is a refined and well-manicured part of Ibiza Town. This private neighborhood, which boasts a playground for the sophisticated and discerning and overlooks Dalt Vila, has established a reputation for combining fine restaurants, lavish amenities, and a vibrant social scene.

Yachting Elegance: A sanctuary for mariners.

Marina Botafoch never lacks a magnificent yacht. Numerous private boats are welcome at its spacious port, including sophisticated motor yachts and grand sailing vessels. This marine refuge has become well-known as a premier option for picky sailors and enthusiasts of the nautical lifestyle.

Boutiques and design studios are high-end fashion destinations.

Along the promenades of Marina Botafoch are boutiques and creative studios that display an exquisite selection of jewelry, accessories, and haute couture. The diverse clientele in this area has made room for both independent and well-known fashion companies to thrive and offer a wide range of designs to suit their interests.

Anticipating Gastronomic Journeys: Savory Cuisine

Marina Botafoch is a gourmet paradise, offering an array of gourmet restaurants and trendy cafes. Travelers are invited to embark on an epicurean exploration journey through this region's culinary sector, where everything from chic Mediterranean bistros to Michelin-starred restaurants offers their own take on cuisine.

A lively atmosphere at night, a spectacular display of nightlife

With the sun setting over the Mediterranean, Marina Botafoch comes alive with nightlife. The opening of swanky cocktail bars, swanky lounges, and swanky nightclubs sparks an evening of sparkle and celebration. An amazing evening is had here thanks to the stylish settings and exciting beats that bring people from all over the world.

Spaces for Art and Culture Galleries and Exhibitions
A creative community exists in Marina Botafoch in addition to its appeal as a posh destination for entertainment. At surrounding galleries and cultural centers, contemporary artists' creations—from paintings and sculptures to multimedia pieces—are on view. These venues offer established and emerging artists the chance to present their work to a distinguished audience.

Calm and Pleasure in Health and Way of Life
At the marina's opulent spas, fitness centers, and wellness studios, visitors can choose from an array of restorative therapies and revitalizing treatments. Marina Botafoch offers a range of holistic wellness services, from invigorating massages to all-inclusive wellness programs, for individuals who favor an all-encompassing approach.

Marina Botafoch is one example of how Ibiza manages to seamlessly blend style and lifestyle. Its elegant shoreline, filled with boats and boutiques, opens up a world of refined tastes and opulent experiences for visitors. With a refined atmosphere that includes fine dining, couture, and bustling nightlife, this rich enclave reflects the vivacious spirit of the island.

Chapter 9. Outings & Day Trips

Day Trips & Excursions: Seeing the World Outside of Ibiza

The stunning shoreline of Ibiza is just one aspect of its charm. Day excursions and travels reveal hidden gems in the area, enticing travelers to see the larger Mediterranean region. Every trip offers a different combination of natural beauty, cultural discovery, and life-changing experiences, from the picturesque beaches of Formentera to the mysterious islets of Es Vedrà and Es Vedranell. These trips provide an opportunity to find undiscovered treasures and make lifelong experiences outside of Ibiza, whether by boat, on foot, or with guided tours.

Formentera Island

Formentera: An Island of Peace and Natural Magnificence

Formentera is a beautiful island in the Mediterranean that is only a short ferry trip from Ibiza. Formentera, a tranquil haven from the hectic pace of its neighboring island, is well-known for its pristine scenery, white-sand beaches, and crystal-clear waters. This is a paradise for individuals looking for a serene getaway because nature rules supreme and there is a sense of peace permeating every nook.

Pristine Seascapes and Beachfront Bliss
Beaches on Formentera are well known, and they can compete with some of the world's most unique beaches. Considered one of Europe's best beaches, Playa Illetas boasts white sands and turquoise waves. With its unspoiled beauty and expansive vistas of the Mediterranean, the nearby strand of Ses Illetes captivates tourists. These beaches provide a haven for swimming, beachcombing, and tanning, as do many others.
Reserves of Nature: Wild Beauty

Formentera has a sizable protected area, which guarantees the maintenance of its pristine state. Salt flats, wetlands, and dunes are all included in the Ses Salines Natural Park, which is shared with Ibiza and serves as a habitat for a variety of bird species. Perched atop craggy cliffs, Faro de la Mola, the island's lighthouse, offers stunning views of the ocean below. The wild splendor of the island is calling nature lovers to explore these areas.

Es Pujols: A quaint seaside town

The principal tourist town of Formentera, Es Pujols, has a relaxed charm all its own. A mix of international and local food is served at the restaurants, bars, and boutiques lining the coastal promenade. The village has a laid-back vibe that makes it a great starting point for exploring the island or just relaxing by the water.

Riding and Investigating: Exploring the Island

Formentera's flat topography and well-kept bicycle trails make it a cyclist's heaven. An enjoyable and environmentally responsible method to tour the island is by renting a bicycle or e-bike. Enjoyable pathways offer a distinctive viewpoint of Formentera's natural splendor as they wind through pine trees, along coastal roads, and to secluded coves.

Boat Cruises and Snorkeling Expeditions: Investigating Underwater

Discovering marine caves, vivid underwater life, and hidden coves is one of the many opportunities presented by boating the coastline. Fans of snorkeling will be mesmerized by the crystal-clear seas rich in marine life. Formentera offers great chances for unforgettable water experiences with guided tours and boat rentals.

Observing the Magnificence of Nature at Dusk

Legendary sunsets over the horizon in Formentera are characterized by a warm, golden glow. Take in this everyday show by staying on the beaches or visiting one of the island's coastline views. Every witness is left with a lasting impression as the sun sets below the horizon, painting the sky in an astounding rainbow of colors.

A haven of peace and natural beauty, Formentera is where the rhythm of life synchronizes with the tides of the Mediterranean. Visitors are invited to accept a slower pace and relish the basic joys of this Mediterranean jewel with its pristine beaches, protected reserves, and quaint communities.

Is Verdà

Ibiza's Mysterious Icon, Es Vedrà

Es Vedrà, a legendary sentinel off the southwest coast of Ibiza, rises majestically from the azure waters of the Mediterranean. One of the most recognizable monuments in the Balearic Islands, this abandoned rock formation has captured the imagination of both locals and tourists for ages with its legend and mystery.

Legends and Folklore: A Magical Source

Myth and folklore abound around Es Vedrà. It is thought to be the tip of the lost city of Atlantis, but other people think it's the Homeric siren's sacred isle. Es Vedrà is said to have magnetic qualities and spiritual importance according to local legend, attracting searchers and inquisitive souls to its shores in quest of inspiration and enlightenment.

Natural Wonders: Geological Wonders and Biodiversity

Es Vedrà is a geological marvel that lies beyond its magical attraction. Made of limestone, this untamed island is home to a wide variety of plants and animals. Along the cliffs where sea birds nest, a variety of marine life, including dolphins and uncommon fish species, can be found in the nearby seas. The island's remarkable and distinctive profile is enhanced by its unique geology and sheer cliffs.

Scenic Vistas: Ethereal Beauty Panoramas

The view of Es Vedrà from the western coast of Ibiza is simply amazing. The island has a captivating silhouette against the horizon when the sun sets, giving it an ethereal hue. Es Vedrà has become a popular destination for photographers, painters, and romantics who want to capture its surreal beauty because of this sight.

Sacred Retreat: A Place of Spiritual Solace

Some people view Es Vedrà as a spiritual destination because of its alluring ambiance. Attractions to the island's coasts include yoga, meditation, and alternative therapy practitioners who come to connect with the island's purported energy fields. Its vicinity is ideal for retreats and holistic therapies, which provide a calm environment for introspection and rejuvenation.

Preservation Measures: Keeping a Natural Gem Safe
A protected nature reserve has been established for Es Vedrà and the nearby waterways because of their ecological significance. By this classification, the island's unique biodiversity is protected and its natural treasures can be enjoyed by future generations. It is recommended that visitors honor the fragile environment and help to keep it that way.

Es Vedrà becomes a symbol of awe and mystique beyond its geological shape. This landmark island makes a lasting impression on everyone it comes into contact with, whether they are exploring it up close, from a distance, or for its spiritual significance. The enduring ability of nature to uplift and enthrall people is demonstrated by Es Vedrà.

Riu Santa Eulària des

Calm on Ibiza's Eastern Shore: Santa Eulària des Riu
Tucked away from the bustling nightlife of Ibiza, Santa Eulària des Riu provides a peaceful respite from the island. Known for its laid-back vibe, gorgeous promenade, and plenty of cultural activities, this quaint

town offers the ideal fusion of Mediterranean beauty and cultural appeal.

Architectural Charms with a Whitewashed Elegance
With its whitewashed homes and winding cobblestone streets, Santa Eulària des Riu radiates classic Ibicencan charm. Ancient buildings and contemporary conveniences are skillfully merged into the town's architecture, which honors its rich past. The town's famous mountaintop church, Puig de Missa, provides sweeping views of the surrounding landscape and is a testimony to the town's spiritual tradition.

Heritage and Art in Cultural Enclaves
The town is home to several cultural attractions, such as the Ethnological Museum, which offers a thorough examination of the customs and history of the island. Santa Eulària des Riu boasts a thriving arts sector that is worth exploring, with art galleries and craft workshops showcasing the ingenuity of regional artists.

River Views: A Beautiful Walk
The town's lovely environment is created when the Riu de Santa Eulària, the town's namesake river, flows through its center. Encouraging strolls and quiet periods of contemplation, a picturesque promenade stretches along its banks. Sleek places to eat regional food and

tranquil views can be found at the riverfront cafés and restaurants.

Coastal Beauty: Beaches and Bays
Some of Ibiza's most serene and kid-friendly beaches are found in Santa Eulària des Riu. Swimming is safe for people of all ages at Cala Llonga because of its soft sand and sheltered bay. Cala Nova is nearby, its vigorous waves luring surfers and lovers of water sports. For those seeking sun, water, and sand, these beaches offer a tranquil haven encircled by hills covered in pine trees.

Gourmet Delights: Adventures in Cooking
The dining scene in the town is a reflection of its relaxed yet sophisticated atmosphere. Mediterranean staples as well as international fare are served in waterfront eateries' diverse menus. Freshly caught delicacies adorn many menus, with seafood taking center stage. Visitors are encouraged to indulge in the island's delectable cuisine by local markets and specialist stores, which offer a taste of Ibiza's culinary legacy.

Health and Leisure: Rejuvenation in the Natural World
A holistic approach to well-being is embraced by Santa Eulària des Riu. Inviting guests to relax and rejuvenate amid the area's natural beauty, yoga studios, wellness centers, and spas provide a variety of treatments and

practices. The peaceful environs of the town offer the ideal setting for leisure and self-care.

With its calm haven and hint of ethnic diversity, Santa Eulària des Riu perfectly captures the spirit of Ibiza's eastern shore. This town, nestled in the soft embrace of the Mediterranean, welcomes visitors to discover a more sedate and contemplative side of the island with its charming streets, beautiful beaches, and cultural enclaves.

Chapter 10: Spas and Wellbeing

Spas and Wellness: Embracing Ibiza's Rejuvenation

The wellness culture in Ibiza is a haven for self-care and renewal. Island experiences for mind, body, and soul include holistic retreat facilities and opulent spas tucked away in boutique hotels. Visitors can indulge in a range of services, including holistic therapies and relaxing massages, all set against Ibiza's stunning natural scenery. Meditation halls and yoga studios offer calm areas for introspection and rest. Ibiza's health offerings, which emphasize holistic well-being, enable visitors to set off on a life-changing voyage of self-discovery and rejuvenation.

Retreats for Yoga

Ibiza Yoga Retreats: Taking Care of Your Body and Soul

Although Ibiza is best known for its exciting nightlife, it also has a calm side that attracts people looking for well-being and inner tranquility. The island's yoga retreats combine the healing properties of yoga with the scenic surroundings and laid-back vibe of Ibiza to provide a sanctuary for introspection.

Escapes that are Holistic: Spirit, Body, and Mind

Ibiza yoga retreats offer a comprehensive approach to wellbeing that nurtures the mind, spirit, and physical body in addition to the former. By utilizing a blend of yoga poses, mindfulness exercises, meditation, and holistic treatments, participants experience a metamorphosis that leads to a restoration of balance both inside and externally.

Beautiful Environments: The Adoration of Nature

Ibiza has a lot of yoga retreats that are thoughtfully positioned within the picturesque scenery of the island. Participants are engrossed in the island's natural beauty, whether they are in tranquil countryside sanctuaries or mountaintop retreat centers with expansive views of the sea. The calm environment provides an ideal setting for introspection and mindfulness exercises.

Skilled Teachers: Advice for Development
Yoga retreats in Ibiza are facilitated by seasoned teachers and practitioners who walk participants through a customized curriculum. The loving and encouraging atmosphere that these knowledgeable instructors provide guarantees that people of all abilities and backgrounds can reap the benefits of yoga.

Diverse Practices: Customized Events
Ibiza yoga retreats provide a variety of practices to suit a range of tastes and styles. Whether it's Hatha, Kundalini, Vinyasa flow, or more specific styles like Yin or Ashtanga, participants can explore and expand their knowledge of yoga in a nurturing and encouraging setting.q

Culinary Delights: the Body A yoga retreat in Ibiza offers a complete experience that includes nutrition. A lot of centers serve healthful, plant-based meals that enhance mindfulness practice while also nourishing the body. Organic and locally sourced products are frequently used, letting guests enjoy the flavors of Ibiza's abundant surroundings.

Connection and Community: Common Travels

Yoga retreats help participants feel connected and as a group. Like-minded people can gather in a supportive environment, exchange experiences, and build deep connections via shared practices, group meditations, and communal meals.

Yoga retreats in Ibiza offer a sacred setting where people can set out on a path of self-awareness, inner serenity, and overall well-being. The transforming power of yoga is enhanced in this tranquil island location, enabling practitioners to rediscover their true selves and achieve harmony amid the breathtaking scenery of Ibiza.

Wellness Centers

Ibiza Spa Resorts: A Sanctuary of Calm and Rejuvenation
The spa resorts in Ibiza provide a haven for people looking to relax, recharge, and treat themselves to the best possible self-care. These peaceful retreats, which are tucked away amid the island's breathtaking scenery, offer opulent lodging along with top-notch spa services, providing the perfect setting for overall well-being.

Holistic Getaways: Taking Care of the Body and Soul
The comprehensive approach to well-being used by Ibiza's spa resorts emphasizes the equilibrium of the

mind, body, and spirit. Customized spa services, healing massages, yoga classes, and meditation techniques are all carefully planned to encourage unwinding, letting go of stress, and regaining equilibrium. Visitors set out on a life-changing voyage of renewal and self-discovery.

Beautiful Environments: The Adoration of Nature
Ibiza has a lot of spa resorts that are well located within the island's breathtaking natural surroundings. Guests are surrounded by the peaceful atmosphere of Ibiza's settings, whether they are staying in beautiful countryside estates or cliffside getaways with expansive views of the sea. The calm settings foster a calm atmosphere that is conducive to introspection and mindfulness exercises.

Top-Notch Facilities: Ultimate Indulgence
Modern amenities at Ibiza's spa resorts are on par with the best in the world. The steam rooms, saunas, jacuzzis, and infinite pools provide visitors with a rejuvenating and restorative sensory experience. Skilled therapists and well-being professionals use a variety of approaches, from conventional to cutting-edge, to guarantee a highly customized and restorative experience.

Gourmet Treats: Fueling the Body and Taste Buds
Ibiza's spa resorts take their dedication to wellness a step further with their cuisine options. Gourmet,

health-conscious cuisines that please the senses and nourish the body include organic, locally sourced foods. The complete spa experience is further enhanced by the delicious meals that guests relish in line with their wellness journey.

Yoga and Exercise: Vigorous Activities in Calm
Many resorts offer yoga and fitness programs that are appropriate for all skill levels in addition to spa treatments. Skilled teachers conduct classes in calm environments where participants can improve their physical health and internal harmony.

Therapeutic Interventions:q Personalized for Each Patient's Needs
The spa resorts in Ibiza provide a wide range of therapeutic services, from conventional massages to innovative therapies. A variety of alternatives catering to specific requirements, such as stress relief, detoxification, or general rejuvenation, is available for guests to select from.

QTailored Encounters
Every visitor's journey towards wellness is specially designed for them. Ibiza's spa resorts place a high value on personalized care, making sure that each visitor receives therapies and treatments that suit their unique preferences and aims.

The spa resorts in Ibiza are more than just opulent establishments; they are havens of well-being where visitors go on life-changing adventures of renewal and self-discovery. With top-notch amenities, knowledgeable therapists, and a steadfast dedication to holistic health, these resorts provide a life-changing experience that uplifts the spirit, mind, and body while embracing Ibiza's unspoiled beauty.

Health Facilities

Ibiza Wellness Centers: Taking Care of Your Body, Mind, and Soul

The wellness clinics in Ibiza provide a peaceful and self-care oasis, offering a wide range of holistic therapies and practices that address mental, physical, and spiritual well-being. Tucked away amid the tranquil settings of the island, these facilities act as havens for people looking for harmony, renewal, and inner serenity.

A Holistic Perspective: Harmony in All Aspects

The holistic approach to well-being used by Ibiza's wellness centers recognizes the connection between the mind, body, and spirit. The physical, mental, and spiritual facets of health are addressed as guests go on a transformative journey that includes therapies including massages, acupuncture, energy healing, and aromatherapy.

Experts in Practice: Knowledgeable Advisors for Well-Being

The practitioners who work in Ibiza's wellness clinics are highly qualified professionals who are passionate about what they do. These professionals use a variety of techniques and customs to ensure that each client receives individualized care that meets their unique requirements and preferences.

Natural Beauty as a Healing Force: Scenic Retreats

Ibiza has a lot of spa facilities that are thoughtfully positioned within the stunning landscape of the island. Whether positioned by the serene shore or tucked away in verdant rural estates, visitors are embraced by the natural world. The calm surroundings offer the perfect setting for introspection, unwinding, and mindfulness exercises.

Yoga and Meditation: Balance and Introspection

In addition to treatments, yoga and meditation sessions are frequently provided by Ibiza's wellness establishments. Guests leave these practices with tools for inner balance, stress relief, and self-awarenesqs. Sessions are guided by knowledgeable instructors in peaceful environments, enabling participants to advance their practice and develop a sense of inner calm.

Dietary Advice: Fueling the Body from the Inside Out

Nutritional advice and counseling are a common feature of Ibiza wellness programs. Professional nutritionists and wellness coaches provide tailored guidance on food selections that enhance general health. Guests learn about mindful eating practices and acquire insightful knowledge about taking care of their bodies on the inside.

Cleaning and Detoxification: Body and Mind Purification

Detoxification programs are frequently offered by wellness clinics in Ibiza with the goal of clearing the body of pollutants and reviving the mind. Specialized diets, fasting, and therapies that assist the body's natural cleansing processes may be a part of these programs.

Meditation Retreats: Life-Changing Events

Certain wellness centers provide guests with the opportunity to fully immerse themselves in a path of self-discovery and well-being through immersive retreat experiences. These retreats offer a comprehensive and life-changing experience, usually combining therapeutic treatments, yoga and meditation techniques, and holistic activities.

The wellness clinics in Ibiza are havens for people looking to reestablish equilibrium, raise their spirits, and improve their general well-being. In the middle of Ibiza's breathtaking natural surroundings, these facilities provide guests with a location to begin a life-changing journey of self-discovery and inner serenity with skilled practitioners, a variety of treatment methods, and a dedication to holistic health.

Chapter 11: Useful Guidance

Useful Advice for Vacationers to Ibiza

Coinage: Euro (EUR)

Spoken: Spanish and Catalan, with a lot of English in tourist areas.

Zone: UTC+1, Central European Time (CET).

Climate: Mediterranean, with warm winters and hot, dry summers.

Power: 230V, plug type F.

For emergency services, dial 112 in all cases.

Transportation: There are plenty of taxis, buses, rental cars, and scooters available. Ferries link Ibiza with neighboring islands.

Safety: In general, Ibiza is safe, however, be cautious in populated areas, especially at night. Observe your possessions and pay attention to your environment.

No need for a visa for residents of the EU. Verify your country's visa requirements.

Health: No particular vaccines need to be obtained. When receiving medical care, EU citizens can utilize their EHIC card. It is advised to have travel insurance.

Atmospheric Conditions

Climate and Weather: Ibiza's Mediterranean Allure

The Mediterranean climate that Ibiza experiences is defined by moderate, wet winters and pleasant, dry summers. An important part of the island's charm is its climate, which offers year-round pleasure, exploration, and relaxation in a picture perfect setting.

June to September is Summer Bliss.

Ibiza's summer season peaks in June and ends in September. Temperatures typically range from 25°C to 30°C (77°F to 86°F), with plenty of sunshine throughout the day. With its enticing warmth, the sea is ideal for swimming and sunbathing. Beach gatherings and outdoor meals are made more delightful by warm nights that keep the fun going long into the night.

Golden Autumn (November and October)

In Ibiza, autumn ushers in a more subdued atmosphere as opposed to the summer's frenzy. The range of temperatures is 20°C to 25°C (68°F to 77°F), with a progressive decrease. Continued beach outings are possible because the sea is still comfortably warm. Rain showers may grow more frequently, but they also add lushness to the terrain, making for a beautiful setting for exploration.

Gentle Winters: December through February

In contrast to many other European locations, Ibiza experiences mild winters. 12°C to 16°C (54°F to 61°F) is the typical daytime temperature; the average nighttime temperature is 6°C to 10°C (43°F to 50°F). There is more rainfall, which revives the island's vegetation. Winter offers fewer crowds and a serene ambiance, making it an ideal season for exploring cultures and taking calm vacations.

March to May is when spring awakens.

Ibiza changes with the arrival of springtime. The temperatures start to increase as the island is awash in vivid wildflowers. Average day temperatures are 16°C to 20°C (61°F to 68°F), with nights being progressively warmer. The return of beach days is signaled by the sea warming. Hiking, outdoor recreation, and discovering the island's natural splendor are all best done in the spring.

Enjoy the Sun: Sunlight Hours

Ibiza receives plenty of sunlight all year round. The island receives about 5 to 6 hours of sunshine each day even in the winter. In the summer, this number can reach up to 11 hours. The island's lively vibe is enhanced by the constant sunshine, which also makes it a popular choice for those looking for some sun.

Travelers can find a welcoming atmosphere all year round in Ibiza because of its Mediterranean climate, which features pleasant summers, moderate winters, and plenty of sunshine. Ibiza's climate is a major factor in its eternal appeal, whether you're lounging on the beach in the summer or discovering the island's natural beauties in the spring.

Tribal Traditions

Local Practices: Adoring the Cultural Traditions of Ibiza

Embracing local customs enhances your experience and creates a stronger bond with the island's residents as you delve deeper into the beautiful tapestry of Ibiza's culture. Here are a few beloved traditions that capture the essence of Ibiza:

Semana Santa: Accepting Leisure and Rejuvenation

Ibiza's way of life is deeply rooted in the siesta, a beloved Spanish custom. Usually observed from early afternoon until late afternoon, companies may close for a short period to give locals and guests a chance to cool off and refuel. Accept this custom by sitting down to a meal slowly, taking a stroll through streets that are shaded, or just finding a peaceful place to unwind.

Fiesta Spirit: Honoring Life's Pleasures

Ibiza's culture revolves around festivals and fiestas. These festivals provide an insight into the island's history, religion, and creative expression, from the exuberant Sant Joan celebrations to the vibrant parades of Eivissa Medieval. You can experience the dynamic atmosphere of Ibiza by taking part in the festivities, whether it is through dancing, listening to music, or eating traditional fare.

Honoring the Environment with Respect for Nature
Ibiza is known for its breathtaking natural scenery, and the islanders have a great regard for the environment. Participate in this respect by choosing eco-friendly activities, saving water, and properly disposing of waste. You may help preserve Ibiza's stunning surroundings by taking part in beach clean-ups or nature reserve explorations.

Taste Traditions: Delighting in Regional Flavors
In Ibiza, dining is an occasion to celebrate community and flavors rather than just consuming food. Take advantage of the tradition of sharing plates, particularly while consuming tapas. Delight your palate with regional specialties such as "flaó," a dessert, or "bullit de peix," a shellfish stew. Enjoy Ibiza's distinct culinary legacy by matching your meals with local wines.

Appropriate Clothing: Grace and Modesty

It is traditional to dress modestly out of respect for churches, especially when attending religious activities or ceremonies. It is advised that both men and women dress in clothing that covers their knees and shoulders. An appreciation of the island's religious legacy and cultural customs is evident in this gesture.

Kind Regards: Accepting Hostility

Ibiza locals are renowned for their friendliness and warmth. A cordial "Hola" or "Buenos días" at the beginning of a conversation not only demonstrates respect but also encourages sincere relationships. Talk to people and welcome the island's welcoming atmosphere without holding back.

You'll show that you have a great respect for the island's cultural legacy in addition to improving your vacation experience by adopting these regional practices. These traditions urge you to become a vital part of Ibiza's colorful tapestry, whether you're enjoying traditional foods or taking part in celebratory festivals.

Money and Gratuity

Money and Gratuities in Ibiza: An Embracing Handbook

Knowing the exchange rates and customs around tipping in Ibiza guarantees a polite and seamless stay. It is possible to express gratitude for outstanding service while honoring cultural customs if you are aware of the local currency and standard tipping practices.

Coinage: Euro (EUR)

The Euro (€) is the accepted form of payment throughout all of Spain, including Ibiza. Transactions are simple and convenient because they may be made with coins or banknotes. All around the island, ATMs are widely spaced, making cash availability convenient.

Tipping Customs: An Expression of Thanks

In Ibiza, leaving a tip is customary but not required as a token of appreciation for excellent service. Here's a general tipping guide for many scenarios:

Tipping is usual at restaurants and cafés, especially for attentive service. Tipping between five and ten percent is customary when dining out. You should feel free to leave a more substantial tip if you experience great service.

Bars: Although not required, leaving a tip is appreciated in bars. A courteous way to thank someone for excellent service is to round up the bill or leave a tiny change.

Taxis: It's polite to round up the fare, though it's not required. Think about staying a little longer if you want great service or help with your luggage.

Hotels: It's normal to tip the housekeeping staff at hotels. It's customary to leave a few euros each night. In addition, you might want to think about leaving a gratuity to express your gratitude to the hotel staff if you experience outstanding service.

Tour Leaders and Operators: If you think the service was outstanding, you should tip for guided tours or transportation services. Starting with a 10% tip is a decent idea, but feel free to change it depending on how satisfied you are and how long the service takes.

Spas and Wellness Centers: Tipping the therapist after a massage or treatment is customarily appreciated. It's common to tip 10%.

Chauffeurs and Concierge: A modest gratuity is a polite way to say thank you for any assistance you receive, such as assistance with luggage or other services.

As always, it's a good idea to use your discretion and base your tipping decision on the level of service you receive. Keep in mind that tipping customs can vary.

You may make transactions easier and express your gratitude for great service by being aware of the money and tipping conventions in Ibiza. The kind words you send back to the island add to its welcoming and upbeat vibe.

Chapter 12: Safety and Health

In Ibiza, Putting Your Health First Health and Safety: Ibiza is well known for its atmosphere, which is typically safe. However, it is advisable to use caution, especially in congested regions and at night. Emergency services can be reached by calling 112. Although EU citizens can obtain medical care with their EHIC card, travel insurance is recommended. No specific vaccinations are required. Although it's easy to find bottled water, tap water is safe to drink. Because of the high levels of sunshine in Ibiza, it's crucial to wear hats and sunscreen. If local COVID-19 regulations—which include mask wear and social segregation—are adhered to, visiting is both safe and enjoyable.

Helpline Numbers

Contact Details: Guaranteeing Security in Ibiza
Knowing the emergency numbers is essential to guaranteeing your security and welfare in Ibiza. The island has services specifically designed to deal with different circumstances quickly and effectively, just like any other resort.

The following emergency numbers are crucial to be aware of:
1. The 112 general emergency number
In Ibiza, as well as in Spain and the EU, this is the universal emergency number. It functions as a one-stop hotline for all kinds of crises, such as fire, medical,

police, and other pressing circumstances. Prepare a description of the emergency and your location before contacting 112.

2. **Emergencies in Medicine:** 061

Dial 061 for medical situations, such as unexpected sickness, trauma, or the need for an ambulance. Skilled medical personnel will evaluate the circumstances and send out the required aid. While aid arrives, they might offer advice over the phone.

Third: Police: 092

To report an event that needs police attention or for non-emergency police problems, please contact 092. You can report events that don't need an emergency response right away or ask for assistance by calling the local police station.

4. **Rescue and Fire:** 080

Dial 080 in the event of a fire or other emergency requiring the fire department's response. Skilled firemen will react quickly to handle the issue and offer the required support.

5. **Marine Rescue:** 112.

To get help in the event of a marine emergency, such as a boat accident or sea trouble, call 112. By calling this number, you can get in contact with the right authorities who can plan maritime rescue missions.

6. **900 123 505 for roadside assistance**

You can get assistance by calling this toll-free number if you need roadside assistance or have automotive trouble. In addition to tire changes and simple mechanical help, they can offer towing services.

7. Poison Information Center: 915 620 420

To report cases of poisoning or exposure to dangerous materials, get in touch with the Anti-Poison Center. Before expert medical assistance arrives, they might offer advice on what actions to take right away.

It is noteworthy that although many emergency circumstances can be communicated in English, it is still necessary to have a basic comprehension of popular emergency Spanish words.

Knowing these numbers for emergencies means you'll be ready for anything that might come up while you're visiting Ibiza. These committed services' timely support and response add to the general safety and well-being of both locals and guests.

Medical Institutions

Ibiza Medical Facilities: Providing Well-Being Away from Home

Offering both locals and visitors a wide range of medical services, Ibiza has a well-developed healthcare infrastructure. The island offers excellent healthcare facilities manned by qualified specialists, whether you need emergency care or routine medical attention.

Primary Care in Public Health Centers

"Centros de Salud," or public health centers, are dispersed around the island and offer basic medical care. General practitioners, nurses, and other medical specialists are available for consultations at these facilities. Vaccinations, common sickness treatment, and basic medical checks are examples of services.

Private Clinics and Physician Offices: All-Inclusive Care Numerous private medical clinics and practices that provide a broad range of medical services may be found in Ibiza. Specialized care in fields including dermatology, gynecology, dentistry, and orthopedics is frequently offered by these clinics. Many private offices have English-speaking doctors on staff, so patients from other countries can communicate effectively.

Hospitals: Emergency and Focused Treatment

Ibiza has two primary hospitals that can handle a variety of medical requirements:

Can Misses Hospital is the biggest and most comprehensive hospital on the island. It is situated in Ibiza Town. In addition to emergency treatment, surgery, obstetrics, and specialist departments for different medical specialties, it provides a broad range of medical services.

Santa Eulària Hospital: Located in Santa Eulària des Riu, this medical facility offers a range of services, such as surgery, emergency treatment, and specialty clinics. Although it is not as large as Can Misses, it is nevertheless quite important for delivering healthcare services to people who live in the northeastern portion of the island as well as tourists.

Apothekes: Easily Available Drugs
In Ibiza, pharmacies, or "Farmacias," are widely accessible. In addition to prescription and over-the-counter pharmaceuticals, they offer professional assistance on healthcare issues. Essential pharmaceuticals are always accessible because of a rotating schedule that guarantees at least one pharmacy is open twenty-four hours a day.

Comprehensive Services for Dental Care
In addition to standard checkups and cleanings, Ibiza dental clinics provide more specialist procedures including oral surgery and orthodontics. To accommodate the various demands of locals and guests, dental clinics that are private as well as public are accessible.

COVID-19 Reaction: Putting Safety First
Ibiza's medical facilities have put strict safety precautions in place to safeguard personnel and patients

amidst the ongoing pandemic. These actions could involve temperature monitoring, mask laws, social separation, and improved sanitization procedures.

Travel insurance that pays for medical costs is advised for visitors to ensure peace of mind in the event of unforeseen health problems.

Ibiza guarantees that locals and visitors alike have access to high-quality healthcare services, which adds to a safe and pleasurable stay on the island. It does this through its well-equipped health facilities and committed medical personnel.

Emergency Numbers: Ensuring Safety in Ibiza

Being familiar with emergency numbers is crucial for ensuring your safety and well-being while in Ibiza. The island, like any other destination, has dedicated services to handle various situations promptly and efficiently. Here are the essential emergency numbers you should know:

1. General Emergency Number: 112

This is the universal emergency number in Ibiza, as well as throughout Spain and the European Union. It serves as a one-stop helpline for all emergencies, including medical, fire, police, and other urgent situations. When dialing 112, be ready to provide your location and a description of the emergency.

2. Medical Emergencies: 061

For medical emergencies, including sudden illnesses, injuries, or the need for an ambulance, dial 061. Trained medical professionals will assess the situation and dispatch the necessary assistance. They can provide guidance over the phone while help is on the way.

3. Police: 092

For non-emergency police matters or to report incidents that require police attention, dial 092. This number connects you to the local police station, where you can seek assistance or report incidents that do not require immediate emergency response.

4. Fire and Rescue: 080

If you encounter a fire or other emergency situation that requires the attention of the fire department, dial 080. Trained firefighters will respond promptly to address the situation and provide necessary assistance.

5. Sea Rescue: 112

In cases of maritime emergencies, including boating accidents or distress at sea, you can dial 112 for assistance. This number connects you to the appropriate authorities who can coordinate sea rescue operations.

6. Roadside Assistance: 900 123 505

If you experience car trouble or require roadside assistance, you can call this toll-free number for help. They can provide services like towing, tire changes, and assistance with minor mechanical issues.

7. Anti-Poison Center: 915 620 420

For cases involving poisoning or exposure to harmful substances, contact the Anti-Poison Center. They can provide guidance on immediate steps to take before professional medical help arrives.

It's important to note that while English may be spoken in many emergency situations, it's advisable to have a basic understanding of common Spanish phrases related to emergencies.

Being aware of these emergency numbers ensures that you're prepared to handle any unforeseen situation during your time in Ibiza. Prompt response and assistance from these dedicated services contribute to the overall safety and well-being of residents and visitors alike.

Health Facilities

Health Facilities in Ibiza: Ensuring Well-Being Away from Home

Ibiza boasts a well-developed healthcare infrastructure, offering a range of medical services to residents and visitors. Whether you require routine medical care or emergency assistance, the island provides access to quality health facilities staffed by trained professionals.

Public Health Centers: Primary Care

Public health centers, known as "Centros de Salud," are distributed across the island and provide primary healthcare services. These centers offer consultations with general practitioners, nurses, and other healthcare professionals. Services typically include basic medical examinations, vaccinations, and treatment for common illnesses.

Private Clinics and Medical Practices: Comprehensive Care
Ibiza is home to numerous private medical practices and clinics, which offer a wide array of medical services. These facilities often provide specialized care in areas such as dermatology, gynecology, dentistry, and orthopedics. English-speaking doctors are available in many private practices, ensuring effective communication for international patients.

Hospitals: Emergency and Specialized Care
Ibiza has two main hospitals that cater to a range of medical needs:
- Can Misses Hospital: Located in Ibiza Town, Can Misses is the largest and most comprehensive hospital on the island. It offers a wide range of medical services, including emergency care, surgery, obstetrics, and specialized departments for various medical disciplines.
- Santa Eulària Hospital: Situated in Santa Eulària des Riu, this hospital provides a variety of medical services, including emergency care, surgery, and specialized clinics. While smaller

107

than Can Misses, it plays a crucial role in providing healthcare services to residents and visitors in the northeastern part of the island.

Pharmacies: Accessible Medications

Pharmacies, known as "Farmacias," are readily available throughout Ibiza. They provide over-the-counter medications, prescription drugs, and expert advice on healthcare matters. A rotating schedule ensures that at least one pharmacy is open 24 hours a day, allowing access to essential medications at any time.

Dental Care: Comprehensive Services

Dental clinics in Ibiza offer a wide range of services, including routine check-ups, cleanings, and more specialized treatments like orthodontics and oral surgery. Both public and private dental practices are available to meet the diverse needs of residents and visitors.

COVID-19 Response: Prioritizing Safety

In light of the ongoing pandemic, Ibiza's health facilities have implemented stringent safety measures to protect patients and staff. These measures may include temperature checks, mask mandates, social distancing, and enhanced sanitization protocols.

Visitors are encouraged to have travel insurance that covers medical expenses, ensuring peace of mind in case of unexpected health issues.

With its well-equipped health facilities and dedicated medical professionals, Ibiza ensures that residents and visitors alike have access to quality healthcare services, contributing to a safe and enjoyable experience on the island.

Claims for Travel Guard

Safeguarding Your Trip with Travel Insurance in Ibiza
To guarantee a worry-free and delightful trip to Ibiza, getting travel insurance is essential. When unplanned events like medical emergencies or travel delays occur, this priceless coverage offers a piece of mind and financial security.

Priority health care is covered by insurance
Essential medical coverage, such as doctor visits, hospital stays, and emergency care, can be obtained with travel insurance. If any unplanned illnesses or accidents occur while you are visiting Ibiza, this becomes helpful. It guarantees that, even while you're abroad, you get timely and effective healthcare.
Emergency and Postponed Travel: Budget Protection
Travel plans may be canceled or interrupted due to unforeseen circumstances such as unexpected illness, family emergency, or travel difficulties. Travel insurance helps you recoup the cost of your vacation by paying for non-refundable costs like airfare, lodging, and other activities.

Protecting Your Personal Property When Traveling with Baggage

Travel insurance covers the replacement of necessary personal items if the luggage is misplaced, broken, or stolen. The impact of such hassles on your vacation will be minimized by packing accordingly for clothing, devices, travel documents, and other valuables.

Lost Connections and Travel Delays: Reimbursement for Losses

You may have to change your travel plans due to missing connections and delayed flights. To guarantee that your trip goes as smoothly as possible, travel insurance covers additional costs, such as lodging and meals, incurred as a result of unplanned delays.

Comfort in Times of Emergency: Emergency Evacuation and Repatriation

Travel insurance covers the expense of medical repatriation to your home country or the closest appropriate medical institution in the unlikely case of a serious medical emergency or evacuation crisis. By doing this, you can be confident that you'll get the care you require at the right place.

Safeguarding Against Third-Party Claims: Individual Liability

Personal liability insurance protects you against unintentional injuries or property damage to other people. It can be included with travel insurance. In the event of unplanned events, this coverage provides both financial security and legal support.

Customized Protection for Adventure Activities and Specialized Coverage

Some travel insurance plans offer particular coverage for travelers taking part in adventurous activities like water sports, trekking, or other specialized pastimes. You will be properly protected for the activities you have selected thanks to this.

Examine the coverage choices, policy limitations, and any exclusions thoroughly before choosing a travel insurance plan. Think about any particular requirements or activities you have planned while visiting Ibiza.

As a wise investment, travel insurance offers crucial security and comfort for the duration of your trip. It guarantees that, even in the event of an unexpected event, you'll be ready to completely appreciate all that Ibiza has to offer in terms of beauty and experiences.

Frequently Asked Questions

Your Guide to Traveling to Ibiza: Frequently Asked Questions (FAQ)

Which Ibiza Travel Season Is Best?

Your preferences will determine the ideal time to visit Ibiza. There is a bustling nightlife and vivid beaches during the summer (June to September). Winter (December to February) is a peaceful respite from the crowds, while spring (March to May) and early autumn (October) offer nice weather.

How Would I Go to Ibiza?
You can travel by air or water to get to Ibiza. International flights into Ibiza Airport (IBZ) are the primary entry points. Ferries, on the other hand, link Ibiza to other islands and the Spanish mainland.

Which Ibiza beaches are must-see?
Playa d'en Bossa, with its lively environment, Ses Salines, with its natural beauty, and Cala Comte, known for its breathtaking sunsets, are some of the well-known beaches in Ibiza.

How Would You Describe Ibiza's Night Life?
The nightlife of Ibiza is well-known throughout the world. Music enthusiasts are drawn to elite clubs, beach events, and DJ sets. The iconic locations are Pacha, Amnesia, and Ushuaïa.

Ibiza Offers Any Inexpensive Places to Stay?
Hostels, guesthouses, and apartment rentals are just a few of the affordable lodging alternatives available in Ibiza. If you want more economical options, think about lodging in San Antonio or Ibiza Town.

Other than partying, what other activities are offered?

An extensive array of activities is available in Ibiza. Indulge in water sports, hike in nature areas, see historical places like Dalt Vila, or simply relax at spas and wellness facilities.

In Ibiza, is English a Common Language?

Indeed, a lot of people speak English, particularly at tourist destinations, lodging facilities, and dining establishments. But locals like it if you know a few simple Spanish phrases.

How is the cuisine in the area prepared?

Mediterranean influences abound in the food of Ibiza. Sample the "bullit de peix" (fish stew) and "flaó" (a dessert), two regional favorites. Diverse gastronomic experiences can be found at neighborhood markets and beachside restaurants.

Ibiza Day Trips: Are They Off?

Indeed, it is possible to go on excursions to natural attractions like Es Vedrà and explore neighboring islands like Formentera. You can also get a flavor of the local way of life by going to nearby towns like Santa Eulària des Riu.

Travelers, is Ibiza safe?

Overall, people think that Ibiza is secure. Nonetheless, take the usual safety precautions, particularly at night and in crowded places. Remain vigilant regarding your possessions and remain cognizant of your environment.

To help you organize your trip to Ibiza, these FAQs are meant to give you important information. To ensure you get the most recent information, don't forget to check for any special travel advisories or advice closer to the date of the trip.

Conclusion

In summary, reveling in Ibiza's magic

You are about to experience a place that goes beyond the ordinary as you get ready to travel to Ibiza. With its sun-kissed beaches, exciting nightlife, and rich cultural legacy, this gorgeous island promises an unforgettable experience that will stay with you for years to come.

Ibiza has an eclectic mix of attractions that satisfy the interests of all types of tourists, from the beautiful sands of Cala Comte to the historic cobblestones of Dalt Vila. Ibiza offers a well-balanced mix of excitement and calm, whether you're looking for heart-pounding pulses at the center of the club scene or peaceful moments in the embrace of nature.

You are invited to enjoy both international and local cuisine in scenic surroundings as the island's culinary landscape takes you on a sensory trip through

Mediterranean flavors. It is a true sense of connection and camaraderie because of the friendly hospitality of the inhabitants and their openness to different cultures and languages.

The feeling of freedom and self-discovery that Ibiza conveys is just as captivating as its physical beauty, as you will experience whether you visit its historical landmarks, partake in water sports, or spend tranquil moments at wellness centers.

Take advantage of travel insurance to secure your safety and well-being, enjoy local cultures, and express thanks through tipping. To ensure that you're in good hands in case of an emergency, familiarize yourself with emergency numbers and healthcare institutions.

Ibiza is, in the end, a tapestry of experiences just begging to be weaved into your very own tale. Ibiza throws wide its arms to those seeking the tranquility of its landscapes or the throbbing excitement of its nightlife. I hope your trip is full of happy, educational, and meaningful experiences that will leave you with priceless memories that are infused with the enchantment of Ibiza for all time. I wish you a safe journey and an incredibly memorable visit to our lovely island.

Printed in France by Amazon
Brétigny-sur-Orge, FR

19722930R00067